The Challenges

of

Masculinity

CARL ERIKSON

authorHOUSE®

AuthorHouse™
1663 Liberty Drive
Bloomington, IN 47403
www.authorhouse.com
Phone: 1 (800) 839-8640

Published by AuthorHouse 10/03/2016

ISBN: 978-1-5246-3998-3 (sc)
ISBN: 978-1-5246-3999-0 (hc)
ISBN: 978-1-5246-3997-6 (e)

Library of Congress Control Number: 2016915196

Print information available on the last page.

Any people depicted in stock imagery provided by Thinkstock are models, and such images are being used for illustrative purposes only. Certain stock imagery © Thinkstock.

This book is printed on acid-free paper.

CONTENTS

IN ONE PAGE

For each man, for you, for me, one of the most persistent questions in his life has been Am I a man, or more likely, am I man enough? For each boy, the biggest question is When will I be a man? Or, What do I have to do to be a man?

Masculinity is the synergistic result of three factors: the abilities, ideas, and actions a male can innately have (tools); the intention with which he uses his tools; and acceptance by his society of his chosen masculinity tools and intentions.

Required Masculinity is the most enforced and expected form of masculinity in our culture. It's also rigid and harmful to men, to people generally, and to communities.

Each of us males in this country must grapple with many challenges in expressing our masculinity:

- Realizing Required Masculinity's Impacts

- Getting Away from Required Masculinity

- Finding your real Self

- Finding your masculinity Tools and Intentions.

- Your emotions

- Coping with conflict.

- Ending your loneliness

- Being a father.

PRELIMINARIES

TO MEN:

The information and ideas in this book are written for you. With this knowledge in your hands, I hope that:

- Each of you will step away from your endless chase to satisfy Required Masculinity, which you're expected to live, and be your own man.

- Each of you will use your own talents and choices to honestly and effectively express your personal intelligence, skills, and values.

- You will raise your boys to be their own men rather than subvert them into the chase after Required Masculinity.

- If you are a government or business leader, you will make decisions not on the basis of "who's man enough" but on the basis of what is intelligent enough, creative enough, and effective enough to build real solutions for business and community concerns.

TO WOMEN:

With the knowledge and ideas of this book in your hands, I hope that:

- Each of you will come to understand the men in your life more clearly and compassionately, particularly the dark stresses they live with to "be a man" by someone else's standards, by Required Masculinity.

- Each of you will step away from men who express the Required Masculinity our culture expects of them and encourage them and your sons to build their own ways of being male. If you were to start saying, "I don't want any part of standard masculinity. I want what's really you," you will give these males powerful permission to question this cultural Required Masculinity and their obedience to it and to make more personal and honest choices for living their lives.

- If you are a government or business leader, you will make decisions not on the basis of "who's man enough", but on the basis of what is intelligent enough, creative enough, and effective enough to build real solutions for business and community concerns..

- You, who are working with men as peers, will increase your understanding of the Required Masculinity dynamics surrounding both of you, help build effective escapes from it, and jointly give respect and attention to each man who expresses his own choice of masculinity.

I suspect that, at more than one point in these pages, you will mumble to yourself, "Does this idiot think that only men face this?" When you do, please remember that this book is totally about men. I am not taking sides in some gender battle here, just trying to stay focused on my topic.

THE WORDS WE WILL USE HERE

We will be using some ordinary words and phrases here in very particular ways.

Competition

dominance competition, a competition in which you intend to gain control over another person, to destroy or reduce that person's self-confidence, or to permanently reduce or abolish that person's power or influence. "Dominance" is used alone sometimes to refer to the same ideas.

testing competition, A competition in which you intend to test your skills against another person or some standard, e.g., a race, an exam, a music competition, a debate, a golf game, who can make the parachute that leaves the egg whole when it hits the ground.

man, male, a human being having male biology and physiognomy.

masculinity, the quality or state that exhibits maleness. Masculinity encompasses the biological basics and the usual capacities and potentials of the general male *homosapiens*.

dominance masculinity, using chosen masculinity Tools to establish dominance over all other people and the natural world and with intent to benefit only or primarily the man's own interests and goals.

personal masculinity, the masculinity Tools and Intentions that a particular male chooses and uses to express his unique Self.

required masculinity, the masculinity endemic in our culture and enforced on boys and men by our culture. The primary Tools of this masculinity are dominance, power, control, wealth, and high sexuality, and its Intention is to benefit primarily, if not exclusively, the man using these tools. A full explanation of Required Masculinity is given below beginning on page 19 and in Challenge #1.

masculinity tools, the abilities, ideas, and actions that a male innately can have and can express or chooses to have and express.

Self, the intrinsic skills, nature, and desires of a particular man.

The Great They, that powerful and inescapable impersonal voice of "they say," "you should," and "That's not right," "What do They expect?" "That's what They want me to do before I get the raise," "They won't like me unless …," "That's the way They think a guy is supposed to be." You know who They are: your boss, spouse, neighbor, friend, girlfriend, parents, siblings, teacher, coach, policeman, fellow worker, anybody. "Do what I ask, and I'll say you're a real Man. Refuse, and I'll say you're a wimp."

I need to say a few words about pronouns. A number of people have argued incessantly with me that this book should be impersonal and objective, and that the personal tone I use diminishes the message. I refuse to change my choice for several reasons. First, we men have been treated impersonally and been expected to act impersonally for our whole lives, even though we have personal lives and want to live our lives personally. Second, the quality of a person's life, male or female, is the most personal thing in the world to that person, and one goal of this book is help men personalize the way they both build and live their lives. Third, in the course of my years of leading men's support groups, it was always one man's story told personally that led another man to grasp a message that really helped him. I never saw abstract talk about deep male experiences move any man to take its message seriously; it usually put him to sleep. So, "I" will be talking with "you," usually in the singular and always personally. For the women reading this, I acknowledge that almost always the "you" here refers to men and not to men and women. Perhaps, however, my "you" is you at an angle, since you can affect how a man in your life deals with masculinity.

IS THIS THE AUTHOR'S PERSONAL STORY OR AN IMPERSONAL STUDY?

It's both. The impersonal part is most of the words you will read.

My "personal" part in this book takes a variety of forms. It forms the motives and foundations for this book. It coughs up examples from my life and the lives of the many men I've known. It certainly created the energy that drove me through the many versions of this book over fifteen years.

In my late forties, I began thinking about masculinity and what it meant. This began primarily because I hadn't ever fit into the Required Masculinity system very well. At that point in my life, I didn't like living it any more and, on several occasions, had paid painful prices for this misfit. I realized more and more that it was forcing me to live for everyone else's purposes and choices and rarely mine. Often, I was unsure whether there was even a "me" here, wherever "here" was. One day in my early fifties, I finally revolted and refused to live this way anymore, and began searching for anything and everything that might help me reach a life I liked better. My searches pushed me again and again up against the expectations of Required Masculinity, what a man is "supposed to be" and must be. In my search, I read a lot of books on masculinity and attended men's groups and men's gatherings.

At fifty-eight I stumbled onto the Men's Resource Center (MRC) in Amherst, Massachusetts, its magazine *Voice Male*, its support groups, and its clear-headed understanding of men and the Required Masculinity vise. I worked for the MRC for seven years, became a volunteer facilitator for its support groups for eleven years, wrote for *Voice Male*, and developed and ran a six-part workshop for men entering the divorce process. The MRC has recently combined with two similar organizations into the Healthy Men and Boys Network (hmbnetwork.org).

Having had my nose pushed in masculinity by all of these experiences and knowing that my personal situation needed answers, analyzing Required Masculinity became inescapable. Once this began, I cracked the iron shell around Required Masculinity and absolutely everything about it fell open to question. Without Required Masculinity, however, I faced a pathless woods of masculinity and having to create a masculinity by myself. In the beginning, Required Masculinity haunted me like an ogre hidden in the trees. Necessity finally forced me to take my first few steps and detours. Once I had taken these, I gained confidence to take my next steps, and my next steps. Four years later, I had discovered a lot I hadn't realized about who I really was and had begun using this knowledge to make new choices of masculinity Tools and Intentions. Finally, it hit me that I had created a Personal Masculinity for myself.

About five years after my first step, I began my efforts to put what I learned about masculinity in these years into this book. Then, I plowed through thirteen years of thought and frustration, five substantial versions of this book, and a couple of plays. The issues you find here constantly waved at me from the many books on men's issues I continued to read. They talked to me whenever I facilitated a men's support group or met a man struggling with his life. What began as the nerve to challenge one bit of Required Masculinity became my right to challenge every piece of it and to demand that Required Masculinity justify why its rules and expectations *had* to apply to me.

I am not a trained psychologist, anthropologist, or neuro-scientist. I'm just a man with a lot of personal experience with masculinity in my life and in the lives of many other men, who has done a lot of reading and thinking about men and their stressful lives. I'm a man who has found different perspectives on masculinity for us to explore. My purpose in this book is to free you from the demands and guilt that Required Masculinity puts on you and to give you the help, permission, and courage to find a masculinity that lets you live the life your heart wants you to live.

WHAT ARE YOU GETTING INTO HERE?

The goal here is to give you permission to search for a Personal Masculinity that you find comfortable to live with and that you believe will let you be the kind of man you want to be. Given the present one-choice-only masculinity you and I face, we're going to travel some roads you may find daunting and surprising.

My apologies in advance, men, for sometimes throwing you into what may feel like Alice's Wonderland. Unfortunately, this is the condition of our subject and most conversations about how human beings operate. My plan is to gradually reduce this Wonderland-ness for you and to lead you into a larger, stronger, and clearer understanding of our subject than you have now. In some places, you may need to give my idea a couple of tries in order to effectively keep the power of Required Masculinity at bay and drag a different perspective into place. Please, trust me and keep at it.

We are focused here on individual men, living their real lives, not lab specimens or some philosophic, ideal man. Unfortunately, the choices and actions and issues of individual men are not simple. To cope with this, we will discuss two kinds of answers. One set of answers are provided by Required Masculinity. While these appear to be clear, precise, and in their view certain, you will quickly discover that they are much closer to propaganda than to solid answers. These Required Masculinity answers should be read like footnotes and explanatory material to our real purpose.

The other set of answers come from outside of Required Masculinity and take many forms. Some of these outside answers are personal answers of particular men I listened to in the men's support groups I participated in or led for many years. In each support group meeting, men talked openly, many for the first time in their lives, about their struggles to live a Required Masculine life when they badly wanted to live a different way. Other outside answers are observations, warnings, and questions I've found in my personal experience and in books and articles (see the Further Reading list at the back) reflecting professional research. Still others may be just explorations, hypotheses, explanations, and options that seem to work well for me and other men. Most of all, these outside answers are a sharing, man to man, me to you, of perspectives and experiences that give a man a guide to a satisfying life outside of the straight jacket of Required Masculinity. Some of these answers may appear new and even shocking or unnatural to you, but they are not idle speculation or treetop dreams. They reflect reported research and what men in my support groups and I have said, felt, and actually done in our own lives.

In a perfect world, I would expand this book to include the ideas and practices of masculinity in other cultures and ethnicities. Although Required Masculinity speaks and acts as if it were the one, only, and universal masculinity, it is not. My inadequate study of masculinity in other cultures leaves me with the impression that men in every culture or ethnicity have masculinity problems similar to those created in our culture by Required Masculinity. In order to bring some simplification to our complex subject, however, I chose to exclude other cultures and ethnicities from our discussion. This omission means that if you want to apply ideas and questions from this book to men and masculinity elsewhere or in the non-dominant cultures in the United States, I haven't given you all the ideas and information you might need there. So, please, go very thoughtfully into those cultures with the ideas I give you here.

HOW TO USE THIS BOOK

Participate

This is your book, your exploration. Use it in whatever ways work for you. When you close the back cover of this book and drop the book on the floor, I just want you to walk away with purpose and confidence in yourself as your own man.

Get out your pen or pencil and scribble in the margins. You have big margins on these pages – fill them up.

Don't just read the words. Kick them around and spar with them. X them out. Underline. Insert "?" and "!" all over the place. Make lists. Jot ideas and more questions down. Come to your own conclusions. Disagree with the observations and conclusions you read. Find your own facts. Maul and mangle these pages. It will take a big mess to free you from Required Masculinity and get you to the man you want to be, so start the mess here.

Questions To Answer

In Appendix 1 you will find exploration questions to jump start your own conversations, explorations, and thoughts. I encourage you to go to them each time you read in this book and put your answers down for whatever questions intrigue you at that moment. Later, go back to these answers and rebuild them, scrap them, refine them. You have plenty of space. Do whatever you need to do to make these questions and your answers useful for you.

Read In Any Order

Appendix 2 is a Topic Index which will lead you to the primary location for a topic. However, male humans are complex, so valuable ideas related to your topic are probably planted in various places in the book and you will probably need to read the whole book to gather everything on a particular topic.

PART 1

WHAT MASCULINITY IS

Even here at the start, we face complexity. We can talk about masculinity in two totally different ways: theoretical and apparent. Like biofeedback, these two invade and affect each other constantly. To begin to understand your masculinity challenges, you need to understand both perspectives on masculinity.

THEORETICAL MASCULINITY

In the very big picture of Life and the World, masculinity is a minor matter. Gender is just a few little tweeks in a gene. In a specific human male, however, it is a very big thing. It affects how his body gets designed and how it functions. It sets much of his psychology. It draws specific demands and expectations down on him. It shuts a lot of doors to him.

Masculinity is best understood as the synergistic creation of three forces:

1. The abilities, ideas, and actions a male can innately have, a man's Tools.

2. The Intention with which he uses his tools.

3. Acceptance or not by a man's society of the masculinity Tools and Intentions he chooses and expresses.

I see these as a triangle. One force on each side aimed at a man in the center. The nature of a particular man's masculinity is the result of how these three forces enhance and distort each other in him or how he lets them do this.

Tools

The Tools a man has to express himself and his life are his innate abilities, ideas, and actions. For the whole of the male sex, these are endless. From boxing to hairdressing. From steelmaking to playing a Stradivarius violin. From nursing to running a multi-billion dollar business. For the individual man, this variety of Tools is more limited but still enormous. So, we're going to start our consideration of "masculinity" with the notion that a man has a huge range of Tools with which to build and express his masculinity.

Not one of these many Tools in its innate form is any better or worse than any other. They each have different effects, and these effects may be more or less desired by the man and the people around him. It's important not to confuse the value of a Tool, say physical strength, with the value of what it is used for. Physical strength can save a drowning child or beat up a neighbor.

Nothing in any of these Tools makes any particular tool the exclusive or nearly exclusive tool of any particular male or any particular group of males. Any Tool can end up in the hands of any male. Similarly, no Tool by its nature is exclusively a male tool. More males than females may use a particular Tool, but this is a matter of individual choices not the result of some inherent element of the Tool.

The Tools available to males, therefore, are neutral, and each male is theoretically free to use any Tool when and how he chooses. One major element of a man's masculinity is the Tools he picks, the abilities, ideas, and actions he chooses to express in his life.

Intentions

The second side of the masculinity triangle is the Intention with which a man uses his chosen Tools. Going back to the example in the Tools section, does he use his physical strength and agility to save the drowning child or beat up his neighbor? In other words, what does he use his Tools to accomplish? Does he use money to buy the protection and comfort of a home for someone, or does he use it to buy a glamorous third home to show off his wealth, or does he use it to buy special favors for himself from the government? Does he fight to protect himself or just harm or belittle someone else?

This Intention can range anywhere from the total self-sacrifice of a Buddhist monk to the egocentric greed of a 1% tyrant. Although Intentions can change from experience to experience, the Intention choices of each man seems to gather pretty consistently around a rather narrow range on the continuum through a month's experiences. A man choosing his own form of masculinity settles on what range on this Intention scale he wants to normally operate.

Acceptance

The third side of the masculinity triangle is social acceptance of the man's choices of Tools and Intentions. While our man can get total control of his choices on the other two sides of the triangle, his choices on this side of the masculinity triangle are down to two: pick to match his society's expectations and demands, or pick his personal choices and cope with the social consequences. Deciding this will probably boil down to finding answers to the following questions:

- How unhappy will I be living my society's masculinity choices which I don't much like?

- How stressed will I feel playing society's man when I really want to be my own man?

- How long will I tolerate doing what They want me to do and think instead of what I want to do and think?

- How much happier will I be living my masculinity choices than living my society's masculinity choices?

It's quickly evident that these questions can only be effectively answered at some point long after a man makes his initial masculinity choices. At the time a man begins making these choices, age nine or ten for most of us, he faces the total abstract question of "me or them" without really knowing the facts. We're children at this point. Society, especially in the form of our parents, teachers, and peers, overpowers us on everything else we're learning, so it does on this masculinity issue, and we end up with its masculinity choices not our own.

These questions, if they get to a man at all, become clear only later in his life. In the experience of the men in support groups and myself, they hit most men in the 45-55 years old range. However, after fifty years of living with the indoctrination and enforcement of the cultural masculinity, few men have enough independence to fairly answer the questions, let alone understand that they have other choices of Tools and Intentions.

The most important secondary purpose of our conversation here is to encourage you to answer the four questions above and, then, to lead you through the screen Required Masculinity has built to make your own choices of masculinity Tools and Intentions.

APPARENT MASCULINITY

As happens with most theories, what's most in front of our eyes can hide a theory if it's persistent and strong enough. In the case of masculinity, the apparent perspective in our culture is Required Masculinity and it does exactly this.

Remember the old story about the fish and his water? He knows nothing about the water because it's just the world he lives in, his "is". We're talking in this book about a man's "is", the thing he lives in but never really thinks about, masculinity. Apparent masculinity is a paradox. On the one hand, like the fish's water, we never think about it. On the other hand we think about it constantly. For each man, for you, for me, one of the most persistent questions in his life has been Am I a man – or, more likely, Am I man enough? For each boy, the biggest question is When will I be a man? Or, What do I have to do to become a man? The answer that comes back from all around us, like echoes in a cave is: Be strong, competitive, in control, hot in bed, and make money, money, money. This Required Masculinity is the water we swim in all the time and never examine.

We men build our life choices to satisfy this masculinity's requirements. You plan your actions so no one will think you're a wimp or a sissy or, worst of all a fag or girlish. How much my boss or our culture listens to me does not depend on how ethical, intelligent, or productive I am, but on how masculine they think I look and act. Others, women included, choose me or reject you by Required Masculinity's standards. Almost everything around us shouts this message loudly, clearly, and completely. Almost every family, community, corporation, entertainment, and governmental voice repeats and repeats its expectations and demands. For most people, for you perhaps, this masculinity is as fixed a concept of life as the color of your eyes or the height of your body. Most men accept its meaning as so obvious, so true, and so normal, that they never think about it.

For many a man, the overwhelming presence of Required Masculinity means having to hourly negotiate a conflict between Required Masculinity's demands and his own good senses and preferences. And, he has to do this within a social context that says he doesn't have a choice, that this masculinity is the only way to be a Man. The insights and demands of the Feminist Movement in the last forty years have increased this two-sided masculinity conflict to a three-sided one by adding its own demands and expectations for maleness. As a result, it's tough trying to be a man in our culture now, and many men feel very uncertain about who they are as men or how to act as men. Some give up the fight and zone out. Others over-masculinize themselves as a way to keep hold of some solid notion of their value and purpose in our culture.

If our fish could stand outside his bowl, he'd certainly see some surprises in the stuff he'd been swimming in all his life. Standing outside our Required Masculinity, you will also see some stuff that might surprise you. You may well be saying to yourself right now, "This guy might just as well question the sun's orbit, 2+2 = 4, or day and night. We all know what masculinity is, and it's as clear as a mountain and just as permanent." And, you'd be right … in some important ways. But, as you have no doubt learned the hard way, an unquestioned acceptance of anything eventually throws you against a wall.

The apparent masculinity in our culture, Required Masculinity, is the result of the three forces we talked about: Tools, Intentions and Acceptance.

Tools

- Men must be in control and push for more control. This control can be in many forms: hierarchical control, physical control (including lethal control), psychological control, financial control, dependency control (make others dependent on you) and many others. Whatever its form, control is always Goal #1 for Required Masculinity.

- Wealth is Goal #2, having bigger and more of everything that costs money than anyone else. Money is the ultimate thing and the ultimate "bigger".

- Sexual activity with women is Goal #3. A sex affair counts more if it is with a woman other men desire.

- Winning is all, and any means is acceptable so long as you win. Losing is not Manly. Not competing at all is girlish, according to Required Masculinity.

- Need no one, never ask for help, and never appear to rely on anyone. Stay lost, ineffective, or injured if you have to. You never admit to any of this, of course.

- Collaborative work looks suspiciously unManly; it looks too much like dependence on another person.

- Men lead, women and children follow in everything.

- Women exist to prove the masculinity of Men.

- Know everything, as long as it's actual or logical. If it's not actual or logical, a Man doesn't bother with it.

- Creativity, emotion, intuition, and spirituality are tolerated only when they produce power and money. Otherwise, they are unManly.

- Showing masculinity is always the priority, regardless of any negative impacts on you or those around you.

- Being a husband and a father is masculine, but only if he expresses these through power, money, and control of women.

- If you can't actually do the Manly thing, act like a Man. Appearing Masculine is more important than reality anyway.

- Everything that is around you must show your Manliness, e.g., clothing, house, amusements, hobbies, voice, gestures, friends, restaurants, vacations.

- If anything in your Manliness creates a problem, use power and money and whatever they can buy to solve it or, at least, to hide it.

- A Man never has a deep friendship with another man; that makes them both fags or girly.

- All males are potential enemies, ready to take what you control, dominate you and demean you. No enemy can ever be a friend or trusted. Even if a male acts like a friend, expect him to turn out to be an enemy in the end. Likewise, you are the enemy of every other male.

- Work, the world of power and money, is the only world for a Man. Only Men firmly expressing Required Masculinity can be trusted in this world. When I'm in this world, I am a Man. "If you're not in this world, you're nothing to me."

- Hide, ignore, or deny everything that is less than totally and obviously part of Required Masculinity.

- Play by the rules of Required Masculinity 100% of the time. 98% is not enough to be a Man.

- To use any tool not on the approved list is proof that you are not a Man.

Intentions

The Intentions of Required Masculinity are clearly egocentric. Any and every Tool is to be used to benefit primarily the Man using it. Exclusive benefits are even better. "I say when." "It's my money." "She's my woman." "I'm going to use that piece of land my way, and you can't stop me." Even when it looks like you're acting for the benefit of others, a Required Masculinity Man makes sure that it increases his power, control, and desirability.

Acceptance

Even a fast look at TV, advertisements, and CEO and political behavior tells you that our culture not only approves of Required Masculinity but demands that every male be fully committed to it. If I don't enthusiastically follow this publicly required behavior, you get, "Wimp," "You're not Man," "You're a sissy," and "You can't trust him to take out the garbage."

How Required Masculinity acquired this immense level of cultural acceptance can be argued from a number of angles. We will shortly explore three of them: Brains and hormones, history, and heroes. None of these theories alone, however, comes close to explaining the whole of Required Masculinity or its pervasive power in our culture. Perhaps, the full explanation lies in the interplay of all of these forces. Without exhaustive research, however, we're never going to get a decisive answer to this question. Explanation or not, of course, you and I, and every man in our culture, still has to deal with Required Masculinity and its cultural support. Nor do these theories give you and me much help in choosing our masculinity Tools and Intentions or in dealing with the cultural forces around us.

Brains And Hormones Explanation

In the neuro-science field, there has been considerable research on the connections between brain structure and hormones and Required Masculinity. The researchers have found that hormones, once they determine the physical sex of a fetus, affect the brain development of that fetus. When hormone levels again rise at puberty, they again affect brain development, though at this point it is less about creating new brain structure and more about intensifying the structure built in the womb. The timing, concentration, and quantity of hormones in a body have significant effects on the relative development of particular skills a brain will develop. Except in extreme cases, no brain skill is ever destroyed or not developed; it's always a question of degree – some people have very effective eyesight and some have less effective eyesight, or hearing, or analytic ability. The hormones creating these effects can be created internally or ingested by the pregnant mother or taken as medicine by the child after birth.

Some people argue that there is a "male brain" and this this brain is the source of Required Masculinity. However, even the brain theory supporters admit that brain configuration does not force a specific action on its body. At best, it only sets up a probability. A human can, and usually will, make different choices in particular situations. He does this by turning on a different part of his brain when his present interests are not satisfied by the pre-set action or the external conditions make the pre-set action obviously stupid or dangerous. If we cut through the gender icing of *Brain Sex* by Moir and Jessel and consider the actual research they describe, the picture changes significantly. This research says (1) the brain has many functions, (2) each of these functions is affected by hormones at its own pace and in its own way, and (3) the effects of hormones are different in each brain due to timing, concentration, and quantity. In the face of these conclusions, it is fair to say that brains in any given group of adults will show a wide range of configurations and operations. Since brain configuration is not controlled by the physical sex of a person, any male can have one of a huge variety of brain configurations, not just a brain configured to process in only the Required Masculinity ways. With all these configurations available, we would expect a man to have a large range of choices for his masculinity Tools and Intentions. In other words, you can follow *your* brain's functions. You can choose the actions *you* want. You can benefit who or what *you* favor. Your choices of Tools and Intentions will get you to the decisions and actions you prefer.

It is even possible to modify the brain configuration that your early hormone experiences set for you. For most people every part of the brain is in working order all the time. Some of yours have been refined and developed more than others so that they dominate the way you think about the world and move through it. Some of them have been left in a dark closet and never or rarely developed or used. It is possible to reach into your brain and activate and develop some of these under-developed functions, just as you learned to play the piano or finally got a decent grade in a math class or learned to get a computer working again. This resurrection takes lots of attention and persistence, and sometimes deliberate training, but you can expand your brain power in new directions whenever you want.

A considerable debate rages over whether the different brain configurations can be called "male" and "female". Saying "Yes, they do" is *Brain Sex* by Ann Moir and David Jessel. Saying "No, they don't" is *Delusions of Gender: How our minds, society, and neuro-sexism create difference* by Cordelia Fine. Compounding the debate is the accepted reality that physical sexuality and brain structure often do not move in agreement. At this point the debate gets very harsh, and charges of "gender bias" and "neuro-sexist" shoot across the table, and the real issues are lost.

Testosterone, a strong hormone in males, is often pointed to as a source of Required Masculinity. It certainly gets much public blame for male physical violence. As far as the researchers can figure out, however, testosterone levels at or near the time of violence have no dependable ability to predict male violence. Christopher Kilmartin, in his book *The Masculine Self*, for example, lays much of the blame for male violence instead on the many violence-encouraging factors in Required Masculinity (Dominance Competition, power, control) and its rejection of emotions and ameliorating friendship.

History Explanation

Two history theories can be built, an ancient-history theory and a modern-history theory.

Ancient-history theory. The ancient-history theory is that men needed to be competitive, violent, and in control in order to survive 50,000 years ago, so this is the way men must be today. To suit this theory's arguments, this date has to be a pre-historic date or a more recent date in some primitive location. With less and less need for these capacities in our present, urbanized, global time, the necessity of this theory has shrunk to fewer and fewer men. The diehard believers, however, argue that these capacities are now locked into every man's historic and genetic memory and are inescapable for every male. Even when this theory had absolute validity, it is doubtful that being a skilled warrior or hunter was ever a fulltime need. Even when skilled hunting or fighting was necessary, a number of the elements of Required Masculinity were not needed or would have been a detriment, e.g., independence, repression of emotion, physical domination of others, sexual prowess.

Sticking to this theory today leads us to an odd evolutionary conclusion. Although almost everything in the natural world has evolved, men apparently shouldn't and can't. Once a warrior, always nothing but a warrior. Once a mastodon killer, always and only a mastodon killer. Granted, some really ancient challenges continue to happen on occasion (wars, attacks, and extreme need for muscle), but the idea that male human beings are the only species in the entire range of creation that shouldn't evolve just because an old capacity is occasionally useful is ludicrous. Men have evolved to build space rockets and Ipads; why not in ways of being male as well? Especially when that evolution would be very beneficial to the man himself and to his community.

This ancient-history theory drops another odd result onto our table. In many ways this theory for Required Masculinity perfectly describes the behavior of the present adolescent male. So, this theory locks male development into the adolescent stage of development, never to mature. How much sense does this make?

Modern history theory. R.W. Connell in his book, *History Of Masculinity*, sees Required Masculinity (not his term, our equivalent of his term) as a uniquely Euro-American creation that acquired its features slowly beginning in the mid-1500s:

- First, the collapse of Catholicism and the appearance of nation states and wide-scale commerce during the Renaissance. This moved the culture from religious organization and purpose to secular organization and economic and political purpose.

- Second, the age of exploration and the creation of overseas empires. This was carried out almost totally by men operating within totally high stress male organizations and groups. These men are the first who behaved close to our current concept of Required Masculinity.

- Third, the growth of cities and commercial capitalism. This gave huge power and status to the accumulation of power and wealth, which were in men's hands.

- Finally, the broad-scale wars that rampaged all over Europe in the 17th and 18th centuries: English Civil War, Thirty Years War, War of Austrian Succession, French and Indian War, American Revolution, French Revolution, and the Napoleonic Wars. By the end of these wars (early 19th century), the masculinity we're talking about had become firmly entrenched in the United States and Europe. Using the empire systems of these countries, this US-European military masculinity slowly forced itself on colonial cultures. We could add that this imposition has been expanded and intensified by global wars and global corporate power in the last one hundred years.

In terms of the United States, I would add another step. For nearly sixty years of the twentieth century, the US was at war, and the draft and the US military had substantial control of the male idea. The military has a precise standard of masculinity, which is nearly identical to most of the elements of Required Masculinity. For the military, these elements often are clearly useful, if not a necessity. The military also has a totally controlled environment in which to train and enforce this masculinity standard directly and indirectly. Having this masculinity laid down so firmly for all of these years, its impact would not easily be erased just because these wars ended. In fairness to the US military, we need to accept that it didn't do this as some sociological or psychological experiment or tyranny to warp the minds of US men. It needed specific kinds of behavior to do its work and simply trained and enforced this behavior in men to get its job done. Even this military explanation isn't very good fit, though, with many of the Tools of Required Masculinity. The vast majority of military personnel are specifically trained to be totally obedient and exercise little independence, but independence is a strong element of this masculinity. Similarly, Required Masculinity's drive for money and power has no place in the military, since there is not all that much money to be earned, and power is granted only very slowly and within a tight, experienced-based hierarchy.

Hero Explanation

One other explanation for Required Masculinity presents itself. The Hero has always been admired, applauded, and sometimes very needed by communities. Once the hero is identified and praised by a culture, it is easy to see how his actions get transformed into an idol. With a hero's strong cultural position, his trustworthy qualities can easily become cultural ideals, then expectations, then requirements for every man in the culture. Or, perhaps, somewhere along the way, hero-worship slid into to the worship of anyone who stands out from the crowd because of the power they throw around, the money they show, or the women they have sex with. Our media's celebrity obsession greases this slide every minute of the day.

The Hero's physical strength and agility, quick decisiveness, command, and control are all part of Required Masculinity. Traditionally, he uses these Tools for the benefit of others. Required Masculinity, however, uses these for the man's benefit and to put down of others, which creates a very different result. This looks like the traditional pattern of a good morphing into an evil. All of this, of course, is just speculation. On the other hand, this Hero explanation seems to give some explanation for the appearance of Required Masculinity and its immense cultural power and influence.

Observations

If you stop and consider the Tools and Intentions of Required Masculinity and their impact on your life or on the lives you know, a number of observations about this masculinity may easily come to mind. Here are some that I have gathered over the years from men in my groups, books, and personal thoughts:

- A man who manages to be mostly Required Masculine we often label "not to be trusted" or even "dangerous".

- Required Masculinity men are expected to be strongly sexual with women, but when a woman says, "No", she challenges his masculinity. These men are supposed to produce many children, proving their sexual power, but only women can bear children, so women control this too. These men are expected to dominate women, but women regularly refuse this domination and walk out. As a result, many of these men can feel powerless in the sexual part of their lives in significant ways and can be angry at women as a result.

- Sex with a woman, for a Required Masculinity male, is not about shared sexual pleasure or an intimate relationship with a woman but about domination and "scoring". Quantity and power, not quality, make a Man.

- Only a dominating heterosexual male can be a model Required Masculinity Man. An impotent male, a celibate male, or a gay male – or even a heterosexual male who doesn't want to control and dominate women – is really not a Man in this scheme.

- Any plan, attitude, action, or perspective is acceptable as long as it shows the man expressing Required Masculinity. Usefulness, honesty, fairness, respect, or even his own comfort are irrelevant.

- Only Superman can be a complete Required Masculine Man. Behavior at any less a standard is a failure as a Man, which means that most men can never "be a Man". One can only wonder how much domestic abuse, child abuse, and cheating is the result of men's frustrations over not achieving this impossibility.

- Because this man sees power and money as the ultimate value, sharing his money and power (e.g., letting his spouse and children use his money and power) is his ultimate gift to them. In giving it to them, of course, he is showing their value to him. It, incidentally, also establishes his power over them, which is always a good thing.

- To build strong relationships with people is to admit dependency on them to some degree. Dependency is unManly.

- All of a Man's time must be spent only in Manly action and thought. Pleasure, contemplation, creativity, health, learning, developing emotional understanding, and play times are not Manly. A real Man doesn't waste his time on these.

- For many of these men, work, the source of their power and money and their masculinity, takes on the aura of paradise or heaven, or at least four gold stars, for a Man. The fact that most men work in circumstances as exploitive, boring, and demeaning as women face doesn't change this attitude. The men also often use work as an excuse for keeping their distance from the emotions of women and children or as a place to flee from unManly demands. This job fixation often turns into workaholism, that very common addiction of men. Since his workaholism is usually rewarded by more money and more power and is socially acceptable, the attractiveness of work rises even higher for him.

- All of the Required Masculinity propaganda argues that this behavior "should be". Normally "should be" is taken to mean that it is the best possible way to think, act, or live. However, ask a girlfriend or spouse who is raped or abused whether Required Masculinity "should be". Ask the victims of playground or corporate bullying whether this masculinity "should be". Ask the employees whose pay hasn't been increased for years so that owners can increase their money pile. Ask the men who have ulcers or die of a heart attack from the stress of obediently chasing power, control, and money for years. Ask children whose fathers give them little attention or abuse them. Ask those who lose because other men manipulate the competition. Ask the communities and environments which have been uprooted by corporate or governmental men throwing around their control and power. Ask the man who wants to be an artist not a truck driver, and the man who wants to be a landscaper not a CEO. What do these contraries do to men's mental, emotional, and psychological balances?

- Domestic violence is not an uncommon action of men committed to Required Masculinity. About one in four relationships experiences domestic violence. It is about the same for heterosexual and for gay relationships although, with many more heterosexual relationships, there are many more heterosexual perpetrators and victims to be counted. By far, most of the perpetrators are Required Masculinity men. Many programs have been established across the country in recent decades to work with men (or is it "on men"?) to prevent these behaviors. Since the statistics don't seem to go down, these treatments apparently have little broad success, although they may succeed with some men. Even one specific success, of course, is better than no successes. The 2014 book, *Voice Male: The Untold Story of the Profeminist Men's Movement*, ed. Rob Okun, presents a fifty-eight page history of these efforts, and its end pages list many organizations dedicated in whole or in part to reducing violence against women.

These and other observations about Required Masculinity are discussed at length in *Stiffed* by Susan Faludi, *The End of Manhood* by John Stoltenberg, *The Myth of Male Power* by Warren Farrell, *Why Men Are the Way They Are* by Warren Farrell, and *Manhood in America*, by Michael Kimmel. Considering all of this, bell hooks in her book, *The Will to Change*, calls this masculinity and its rules and expectations the single most life-threatening social disease assaulting the male body and spirit in our nation. And, I'm sure you have your own observations to add to this research.

Change

Required Masculinity has a long history in our country and a particularly strong one since about 1850. Much was written and spoken in the men's movement between 1990 and 2005 about "redefining masculinity," usually with accompanying smiles of good intention. I'm sorry to report that, when I was active in the movement in these years, I saw no real change in Required Masculinity accomplished. No political-legal-publicity campaign to change the demands of this masculinity was remotely equivalent to the size or effectiveness of the feminist campaigns in the 1970s and 1980s. Nor have I seen serious attempts to actually redefine Required Masculinity in any of the many books and articles on men's issues that I have read since.

Is a redefinition of Required Masculinity possible? In an abstract sense, anything is possible. However, we're talking about major social change here. To make this change culture-wide, we face a powerful and broad opposition, both active and passive: the deep philosophical, religious, corporate, political forces and habits that support and train men into this masculinity. In a real sense, then, an effective redefinition of Required Masculinity seems totally unlikely. We might just as well try rebuilding a jet plane in mid-flight or an aircraft carrier while it's caught in a typhoon.

If you can't break the hold of some enemy if he gets you, you'd better get another plan in gear. So, maybe we should launch a guerilla attack instead and keep it going for a long time: breaking the hold of Required Masculinity man by man. One man at a time steps away from Required Masculinity, turn his back on it, and finds and expresses his Personal Masculinity. And, we raise boys fully aware of the meaning of the elements and force of Required Masculinity, teach them how to find their Personal Masculinities, and give them our protection to stand against its propaganda and the bullying that enforces it. Much of this book is devoted to showing you, your sons, and your brothers ways to do these. Given the benefits that come from leaving Required Masculinity and claiming their own masculinity Tools and Intentions, I'm very confident that each of you can improve your life and the lives around you by claiming your Personal Masculinity. Then, maybe over a couple of generations Required Masculinity will lose its power and control over men.

CURRENT HARD MALE CONDITIONS

Various books and articles over the years have put forth many statistics pointing to a number of hard conditions that many men live with. I hesitate to pass them along, but they point out some important pieces of the world in which men have to live. It has been difficult to update or independently confirm many of these statistics, so I urge you to take them only as relative measures of each condition rather than as specific measures of a condition as of 2016:

Lower Life Expectancy. On average, white females live until 81.3, white males until 76.3 (2009). This gap is larger in other ethnic groups, but men always have the lower life expectancy.

Prone To Developmental Disorders. Boys are many times more likely than girls to development disorders like autism and dyslexia.

Higher Suicide Rate. The suicide rates of boys and girls are approximately the same at age 10. The boy suicide rate climbs rapidly until it reaches five times the girl rate at age 19, the point at which boys face the greatest pressure by Required Masculinity. The male suicide rate for all ages is four times the rate for females. Suicide is the second leading cause of death for people 15-34. In general, it is the seventh leading cause of death for males and the fourteenth for females. (2015) We're talking about successful suicides here.

High Crime Victim Rate. For years men were more likely than women to be the victim of a violent crime (even when rape statistics are included), but the male victim rate as of 2008 had fallen almost as low as the female victim rate. Men, however, are three times more likely than women to be murder victims. (2008)

War Casualty Rates. 98.4% of the United States troop casualties in Iraq were men (2010).

Extreme Occupational Risk. 93% of occupational deaths are male (2013). The five most hazardous jobs in the United States are filled by men 97% - 99% of the time.

High Health Risk. Twice as many men as women will die of coronary artery disease, similarly for cancer. Some of the writers I read claimed that, in the ten most common infections, men are likely to have more serious encounters in seven of them than women.

Homeless. 75% men (2013).

Imprisoned. Men are 93.3% of the people under correctional supervision (2016).

Subject To Death Penalty. A man arrested for murder is many times more likely to receive the death penalty than a woman convicted of murder.

Growing Lack of Education of Men. High-school boys of college-educated parents score 25% "below basic" on a major reading test; only 7% of the girls scored this low (2012). 22% of boys drop out of high school before graduation; 15% of girls do (2012). Only 78% of boys who start high school graduate; 85% of girls do (2012). College enrollment is only 38.3% male, even though the male and female populations are approximately equal at that this age

(2012). Males receive only 41.3% of all degrees, and the rate is even less at the Associate and Bachelor degrees level. Taken together, these statistics show men being left with significant education gaps.

Infertility. Male infertility occurs as often as female infertility (2002).

Life Stresses In Marriage. Some researchers (unidentified) named ten "life strains" that increase stress for men. All ten are increased by marriage.

Individual stress. In the men's groups I joined and in the ones I led, men regularly talked about:

- I'm lonely. I don't have a real friend.

- My own emotions scare, terrorize, or unstable me.

- I feel incompetent to deal with conflict in my office, community, and family. Beating people up or humiliating them doesn't settle the conflict, but I don't see any effective options.

- I have a really tough time relating to my kids, except as disciplinarian or money bag.

Decline in public presence. In the last few years, it has become more and more noticeable that there are many fewer men in their expected places in offices, stores, public transportation, lunch-time restaurants, and many homes.

Hanna Rosin discusses this phenomenon in her book, *The End of Men and The Rise of Women* (2012). Don't let the last half of her title scare you off; the masculine half of her book is useful to us here. In it, Rosin provides a number of surprising statistics that quantify this situation. The two most interesting are:

> Twenty percent of men are no longer working. The pre-dominant current explanation of this situation is the major disappearance of factory and middle management jobs and the rise of jobs needing advanced academic training and people skills. The withdrawal of many men from higher education leaves them without the training. A big mystery in this is why so many men have refused to retrain themselves to acquire the needed new skills or to adjust their goals to meet the requirements of the new jobs coming on line.

> In all but three areas out of two thousand metropolitan areas in a survey, young women had a median income higher than that of young men. Rosin provides a number of interview quotes from women who refuse to marry, because they can't find a man earning as much or more income than she is, but intend to have children and lead single parent lives.

A dubious, but possible, explanation for this male disappearance slowly gathered strength for me as I was finishing this book. Many men are exhausted and bored by Required Masculinity and its mostly unachievable expectations. Each man, in a crude and not very useful way, is giving the finger to the Required Masculinity that our society requires but is at a loss for ways to build himself and claim his place in the world. While walking out of the world isn't very sensible long term, it's understandable as a reaction to Required Masculinity.

A large portion of this male disappearance, of course, is also explained by the male homelessness, suicide, and incarceration rates I gave above.

From these hard male conditions, it is pretty clear to me that vast numbers of men, even with all of the money, power, and women that Required Masculinity gives them, are not happy, healthy beings in many ways. It is impossible, of course, to determine exactly how Required Masculinity and each of these conditions interact. On the other hand, human beings rarely act or respond on a single track; we function in a constant input and feedback system, and the Required Masculinity system is a big part of a man's input and feed-back system. It seems highly likely, therefore, that these conditions are connected in some ways to the operation of this masculinity. What these precise connections are I do not know, but here are some strong possibilities:

- Required Masculinity behavior produces or leads a man into situations that cause the harmful conditions.

- This masculinity persuades men that many otherwise useful activities are useless if not "bad", e.g., education, health care, creativity, friendship, compassion, sharing.

- Living in any harmful condition raises a high level of frustration, anger, or fear. The lack of emotional understanding and training caused by Required Masculinity leaves a man incapable of responding effectively to these emotions. This masculinity gives him only violence as an emotional outlet, which of course leads to more harm than good.

- This masculinity has long denigrated skills not demanded by Required Masculinity as womanly and bad. So, men feel more manly by avoiding these, even though they lose a lot of benefits.

The combination of Required Masculinity and the conditions we just discussed create the world in men in our country have to function. This is a far from easy world and one which more often than not forces a man into a box he doesn't like. To cope with this and, better, to climb out of it, he faces some big challenges.

PART 2

MASCULINITY CHALLENGES

Every male in this country must grapple with many challenges in finding and expressing his masculinity. I feel boxed in. You sense that you're losing yourself. I find myself doing things that the real me doesn't agree with. You can indulge in your artistic skills only hidden away from The Great They. I can indulge my love of bird watching only on private occasions or when I'm traveling in Lithuania.

All of this adds up to a large burden of stress on our lives that we certainly don't need or want.

CHALLENGE #1: REALIZING REQUIRED MASCULINITY'S EFFECTS

By far the largest and most difficult challenge for a man is to understand the grip of Required Masculinity and its effects on his life. This challenge focuses on the harms it causes a man, those around him, and his communities and on the cultural pressures forcing him into obedience to its rules and, therefore, to its effects.

This masculinity and its strong enforcers, The Great They, argue strongly and loudly that living according to its expectations is the only thing that can bring a man a life as a male, and that all is sunshine and flowers in the land of power, money, and Dominance Competition. All is wonderful. All is perfect. "'Tain't so, McGee," as a very old radio show used to say. "Not so," would most of my men's groups say. It was the negative impacts Required Masculinity quietly dumped on my life that drove me into the study of this masculinity and writing this book. It's time to get these negatives out of the dark and onto the table, so all of us can see them clearly.

The Harms

Here are the harms of Required Masculinity that men have named for me, that I have felt myself, and that books cite. I've grouped them by who bears the biggest impact of each of them:

To us directly:

Puts you at risk.

Inconsistencies create enormous stress.

Individual thoughts and choices are excluded.

Isolates you.

Causes or contributes substantially to my mid-life crisis.

<u>To us in our relations with people close to us:</u>

Obstructs relationships.

Keeps me focused on Required Masculinity rather than on family and friends.

Prevents you from trusting people around you.

<u>To you in your connections with your community:</u>

Permits only one type of male.

Enables The Great They system and its consequences.

Reduces considerably the attention paid to community and social considerations.

Lacks ethical values.

Excludes many needed skills, attitudes, and goals.

Discriminates against men who express masculinity in other ways.

Creates bigotry.

Of course, not every male experiences every one of these impacts in an extreme way or perhaps at all. But, as long as a man operates predominantly within the terms of Required Masculinity, however, he almost certainly will face most of these impacts to some degree.

Harms Us Directly

Hidden among the power, sex, and money that Required Masculinity promises to men are some undesirable gifts. After research, the American Psychological Association pointed out that the "… traditional male role – which restricts emotional expression and encourages a pre-occupation with success, power, and competition – is associated with negative physical and psychological consequences …" (2014). These various consequences come in many forms and from many directions.

Puts you at risk

Limited Life Choices. Women have three socially acceptable life options (work fulltime, mother fulltime, and some combination of these two); You have only one approved choice (earn power and money fulltime).

Caught Between Two Masculinities. Movies, TV ads, and TV programs (the most pervasive presentation of "male" in our culture) swerve wildly from exaggerated Required Masculinity Tools and Intentions to you as a dumb muscular robot, failure, and jerk. Pulled in two directions by these messages, you have to struggle to find a stable and dependable masculinity.

Left Unprotected And Unsupported. In most crisis situations, you are expected to stand alone, depend on no one, take care of yourself. A woman, on the other hand, will be shielded, protected, and supported. You go down with the ship; she gets in the life boat and collects your life insurance and Social Security benefits. When was the last time you heard someone say, "It's not right to hit a man"? Yes, men do "circle the wagons" and protect each other on occasion, but rarely in anything less than a life or death crisis. What is the thing a man most wants in a male friend? "He'll protect my back," a desire not often achieved since depending on someone else is not Manly.

Inconsistencies create enormous stress. Required Masculinity is full of inconsistencies and creates more when it bumps into the real world. They touch fundamental issues and feelings for us. These inconsistencies come in three primary types:

Required Masculinity vs. Being The Man Who Is Me. To make our contract with Required Masculinity as a kid, we almost always had to repress our Selfs, the persons we naturally were, in order to meet the standards and demands of this masculinity. Since then, we've tried (dare I say "manfully"?) to keep our Self repressed. Our Self, however, usually refuses to die. It keeps operating and regularly commands our attention. We all know That Voice, the one that stands up to Required Masculinity, denying, questioning, and challenging it. "Was that really necessary? Wouldn't I have felt better if I'd been nicer (more generous, kinder, more respectful) back there?" This masculinity tells us X; our Self growls and pokes us in the ribs and says Y. Usually X and Y are very different in intention and impact. Which do you go with? This is rarely an easy choice for us; both have prizes and punishments. Often, it seems to boil down to who's the biggest pain in our ass at that moment, the voice of Required Masculinity or the voice of me.

Males, as children and young men, have a natural habit of straight talk and honesty. Required Masculinity, however, says honesty never wins, so use deceit, misinformation, and backstabbing and you'll win. It also says never, never challenge the rules of Required Masculinity, even when they are producing damage, problems, and stress for you.

Required Masculinity vs. Required Masculinity. This masculinity is glib about demanding one thing and then, by some other rule or expectation, making that thing difficult to achieve. Here are a few of the more obvious of these incompatible demands:

- Be independent. But, to acquire and keep money and status and power over others, we have to obey those who hold control over us.

- Women, marriage and family are essential. But, most activities praised by this masculinity, e.g., business, war, power, require actions that separate us from family and women, e.g., constant business travel, 18-hour work-days, years long absences, and constant business cellphone calls during family time.

- Women are essential possessions. But, this masculinity derides everything that is or appeals to the feminine, i.e., that which would make a woman comfortable or welcome.

- We must have power. But, Dominance Competition insures that few of us will get real power, since there can be only one of us at the top. So, all the rest of us are failures and not Men to some degree.

- Play by the rules of Required Masculinity, and the rewards are mine. But, the rewards appear and disappear at the whim of The Great They depending on whether They decide I am a man or as a sissie or fag. But, I never get to be a man once and for all, since the tests for this masculinity go on forever.

Required Masculinity vs. Reality. Since this masculinity does not control reality (although it works hard to do so), its demands are often rendered impossible by the reality of life, the world, and other people.

- "Dominate."

  But, women hold a lot of power in the sexual field and others control the power in almost everything else. Since most of us men usually can't exercise the needed power, it's easy for many of us end up feeling substantially powerless. Do we resort to violence to prove our power?

  But, almost all jobs and relationships require skills other than power, control and sex to achieve pay raises, the corner office, good feelings, and a solid home life.

  But, every human being wants and needs social connection.

- "Obey my rules."

  But, many ads, TV shows, and movies show us males as dumb, thoughtless, and hopeless, particularly when the guy is functioning closest to the Required Masculinity model.

  But, many Required Masculinity groups (military, team sport, police, corporate) actually penalize independence and Dominance Competition within the group.

  But, many rewards are actually under the control of women, the economy, politics, weather, or the times. None of these pays much attention to the rules or promises of this masculinity.

- "Marriage and family are important."

  But, women and children fail to give us what is important by Required Masculinity standards, e.g., dominance, control, and wealth.

  But, the laws and courts do little to protect your family position at the

  time of family crisis or divorce.

- "We should compete for women and rule them." But, on the very first date, we discover that women are independent, hold real power over sexual access, and want something different than to be a sexual conquest.

- "Women will come to the male who lives by the rules of Required Masculinity, at least to the man who gets the power and money rewards." But, even a woman whom we attract by living the terms of this masculinity often leave us, hurling complaints about the very attitudes and behaviors that got us the power and money that attracted her.

- "Great power and big money make a successful life." But, our day to day, actual, life is filled with everything but power, money, and control, and the hassles that really bother us usually have little to do with any of these.

- "All real rewards come by living this masculinity."

  But," the media laughs at us, my minister lectures us, and organizations run campaigns against us when we chase and exhibit power, control, money, and sex.

But, we get more satisfaction from sailing, vacationing with my family, or building a piece of furniture.

- "Friendships with other men are dangerous and unManly."

But, our best memories are often of the boys and men we've played with, worked beside of, or helped.

But, we can accomplish very little towards all that money and power, or in our relationships, or in the community without the cooperation (i.e., friendship) of other men.

But, we often find ourselves isolated or lonely, turning to women for friendship is taboo; we can only have dominating sex with them.

- Required Masculinity says "Compete to win," but most of us happily cooperate most of the time. It says, "Dominate," but most of us don't dominate and find Dominance Competition exhausting and often rather silly.

- It says, "Women are inferior," but we love women and respect them and their ideas and actions.

- Required Masculinity says, "Don't cry. Don't feel." But we have emotions all the time, and you and I know it.

These various inconsistencies surrounding Required Masculinity, like all inconsistencies in human experience, cause uncertainty, frustration, and stress. Do they also lead to loss of sleep, confusion, anger, depression, and any number of disruptive psychological, relationship, and addiction consequences? The experts seem to agree that stress can be a significant cause of ill health, psychological issues, and addiction but say little about the sources of this stress. In my men's groups, I heard many men talk about how these inconsistencies and conflicts added stress to their lives. Do they play a significant role in the physical and other negatives you or I live with? I also suspect that these inconsistencies play a significant part in the chaos of our mid-life crises. How much domestic violence do you think that these inconsistencies lead to? Violence and anger are pretty common responses of men to frustration and confusion, so ...?

Individual Thoughts And Choices Are Excluded. Required Masculinity sets out a very specific set of rules and concepts. These are not chosen by me; they are imposed by cultural force and the enforcement of Required Masculinity or by The Great They. These rules do not reflect your nature, nor do they reflect how you and I see the world or want to interact with it. Required Masculinity is set up as the only masculinity rule, so each of us men must comply. Extreme training and enforcement mechanisms (see the next section of this Challenge) are rigorously used to make sure that I don't step out of line and you don't even think your own thought. Of course, all such a system can produce, then, is a line of robots.

Required Masculinity tries to be 100% of our thoughts and actions, the more habitual the better. This leaves no free time for me to have my own thoughts and make my own choices or the space in which to practice them. Usually Required Masculinity takes over before a boy even has time to discover himself or develop the discoveries he does make into practical action. Only a very rare or upset young man, who also has a lot of guts and stamina, will fight the system of this masculinity and make the time for his own being. One of the strange things about this closed world of Required Masculinity is how often the very power and wealth it demands are destroyed by the very things it creates: group think, mindless obedience to power, and not listening to the out-of-step viewpoint.

Isolates You. One major effect of Required Masculinity's demand that you be independent and have no reliance on anyone else is to push you away from family, friends, and colleagues even when you could benefit from the connection or need help from them. This effect shows up in various ways:

- Loneliness.

- Lack of intimate relations with family, friends, and associates.

- Lack of a male support network. Women are known for their network of girlfriends, the women they to turn to in times of stress and uncertainty. This provides them valuable information, encouragement, approval, and a sounding board to test out their ideas and choices. At best, your network probably consists solely of a spouse or partner, and even this is usually of little help since you've been trained to reveal no fear, no frustration, no personal wish and told not to rely on others.

- Discourages me from seeking professional assistance in many cases, particularly medical and psychiatric care. We men are famous for not showing up in doctor and dentist offices until our conditions are dire.

Causes Or Substantially Contributes To Our Mid-Life Crises. Women snicker about our "mid-life crises",

53

our children are baffled by them, and our friends are often appalled by them. But, almost every one of us over fifty understands that this is a real crisis. Purpose, capacity, and self-confidence have suddenly disengaged. I used to act with purpose, now I flounder. More money, a step up the ladder, and fancy titles have lost their power to move us, sometimes even to keep our respect. Doing anything else feels a lot more attractive than making the next meeting, deadline, or quarterly bonus. Going out with friends becomes just "doing it again" and again. We feel lonely at home, at work, and almost everywhere.

Somewhere in our forties or fifties, each of us is forced to face some unhappy facts about our efforts to live up to the demands of Required Masculinity:

- I'm not the stud I'm supposed to be and am never going to be him, so I'm less of a Man.

- I'm not Superman; I'm a hack in the back office. I'm never going to get to the corner office, and the new man – or, more likely these days, the new woman – is now the pampered "Golden Boy". So, I'm less of a Man.

- Work is rarely as exciting as I was led to believe it would be. Mostly it's running around the same old circle for the 417th time, and I don't find much challenge or pleasure in any of the circles. So, I'm less of a Man.

- The promises of glory, money, and power that Required Masculinity made to me twenty years ago have turned out to be lies. I don't get much or any of that stuff. Almost all of it goes just to the very few at the top and their cronies. If I'm one of these,

I sometimes wonder if this stuff is worth the price I pay. So, I'm …

- Even what little money and power I have doesn't seem to get me much but stuff. My wife controls my home life and says "No" in bed. My kids ignore me and see me only as a checkbook or executioner. Everybody has got their hands out. My neighbors complain because I don't mow the lawn often enough. Airports and hotel dinners bore me to death. So, I'm …

As this Required Masculinity cracks and fails around you, your very definition of yourself as a man starts cracking and failing, too. Is it any wonder that you feel like a train whose engine has disengaged? To pursue the "engine" analogy, it's as if the locomotive pulling you has uncoupled your car in the middle of nowhere and gone on its way. You discover that you're sitting on the track with no way to go. Even worse, you're sitting on a track with a downward slope, and you're moving down it without any way to control where you go or how fast you move. Should it be a surprise that these loose "cars" run off the tracks often, especially on the curves produced by job loss, divorce, illness, or financial disaster?

Harms To Us In Our Relationships With People Close To Us

Obstructs relationships. To be satisfying for any person, a relationship needs to be built on equality of respect, sharing, interdependence, and emotions such as compassion and love. But, these elements are specifically contradicted by the demands of Required Masculinity: independence, control, Dominance Competition, no emotions, and sex as the only object of a relationship with a woman. How can any effective relationship be built on these bases, let alone a close and dependable relationship with a woman? Yes, a man can have a master-servant, master-slave, leader-follower relationship this way, and men certainly have had these for centuries. However, women and kids talk at length about the costs they pay when living with this kind of husband or father.

Much of the change brought by the Feminist Movement was aimed at breaking these kinds of male-female relationships. The goal was to change our culture so that male-female relationships were built for both men and women, and substantial change has been made. Unfortunately, Required Masculinity has not budged an inch in its demands. As a result many men have not substantially changed, or they feel that they cannot change and remain Men, and some feel themselves jerked back and forth between the demands of this masculinity and the benefits of improved relationships with women. A few men, willing to risk their status as Manly, have stepped away from Required Masculinity demands and built better relationships with women, their family, and with other men.

"Aha," I hear you say, "I've got you now. The sports team works. The military team works. And, these guys are totally Required Masculinity types." Before you break out the champagne, please, take a second look at your teams. Independence is forbidden in both; each man is trained to do only as he is told. Anyone who interferes with the role each is expected to play or with the coach or general is thrown off the team or severely punished. Dominance Competition within the team is ruthlessly repressed; in fact, nothing destroys athletic and military teams faster than men who compete this way with their teammates. Where's the sex with women on team time? Where's the money in most teams? Where's the "power over others" for most team members? These are all pieces of the Required Masculinity model, but they are banished from your teams. I agree that these teams are praised for being models of Required Masculinity but, looked at closely, they begin to look more like massive exceptions to Required Masculinity, or maybe it's hypocrisy.

If you want to see relationships of men in a more real environment, look at teams in the business and corporate spheres. Corporations have a notoriously tough time getting their teams to function. More often than not, Required Masculinity demands take over, and the teams either explode or turn into group-think exercises. A real team is one in which the real and individual skills and ideas of each member of the group have equal status, but this equality cannot exist when one member always carries the right to tell you, "You're not a Man, you're a sissy" and insists on controlling the group.

<u>Keeps a man focused on required masculinity</u>. To satisfy the demands of Required Masculinity requires all my time, energy, and attention. This is not just about a couple of parts of my life. It's about my every thought and action. It's about making sure that everything I touch or affect fits the demands of this masculinity. The most feared statement I can hear about myself is, "He's no Man. He's a wimp." You are not supposed to see the world on your terms, but on Required Masculinity terms. You are not supposed to create a relationship with a wife on your and her terms, but on Required Masculinity terms. You are not supposed to live with your children on their terms, but on Required Masculinity terms. It's the same for relatives, friends, and neighbors. Unless they fit into the power, control, Dominance Competition, and money obsession, then these people are irrelevant to your life as a Man.

Prevents a man from trusting people around him. If a man is supposed to be in control, not dependent on anyone, and in Dominance Competition, where is there room for trust? Trust means that I'm going give up some of my control to Bill. It means I'm going to depend on Bill for things. It means that I'm letting Bill play the game his way as much as I get mine. And Bill does the same for me. Required Masculinity absolutely forbids all of this. Without trust, what chance does a company, community, or nation have to survive and prosper? That so many do suggests that many men evade Required Masculinity and its demands a fair amount of the time, and that this masculinity is not as powerful and absolute as it likes to claim. Here's another sign that you can walk away from it.

Harms To Us in Our Connections With Our Community

Permits only one type of male. All of the messages and enforcement tools of Required Masculinity drive toward creating only one type of male, the male fully committed to and expressing Required Masculinity. Any other kind of male is subjected to a battery of attacks, humiliations, exiles, and punishments. We end up with a totally homogenous male culture, all of us acting, thinking, choosing, and acting with the same Tools and Intentions. No doubt this has its conveniences for some, but it's of very questionable value to our communities and easily becomes a short road to disasters.

Only one range of knowledge, standards, and perception operates in the Required Masculinity culture. Only one range of answers will be considered and used. Only one set of intentions will be given space or supported. This is group think with all of its usual problems. Also, when these Required Masculinity answers fail in a given situation, as they often do, our culture usually sees just one option: go on using the failing knowledge, intelligence, actions, and intentions again, and again (repeating the failure, of course). Consider the Palestine-Israel conflict, President Bush's Iraq and Afghanistan wars, the 2008 financial collapse, the automakers refusal to act on mass model failures. They are all heavily driven by the mind-lock of Required Masculinity. Expecting success from a process that fails so often doesn't look very smart or sensible.

Enables The Great They system and its consequences. First, a quick review of The Great They system. Required Masculinity says that you can be a man only if you act and think in specified ways. Who determines that you act and think this way? They, "The Great They" in my terms, and that's nearly everyone around you. They are free to make this determination all the time, any time, and for whatever reason. If The Great They approves your action, They give you the power, wealth, sex, and the rest of the rewards. If The Great They disapproves of your action, They withhold the rewards of power, money, and women and call you "wimp", "mouse", "nincompoop," "girly".

One significant consequence of this situation is that you and I become dependent on the opinions and desires of The Great They. We define our lives and sense of satisfaction by Their opinions. The skills and talents we use are determined by our employers. Our personal lives are determined by the expectations and demands of wife and children, parents, or teachers. My philosophic and spiritual life is determined by my church. Your social life is determined by your employer, wife, beer buddies, neighbors, and the media. My intellectual life is determined by my schools and the TV I watch. Your political life is determined by the opinions of the media and your neighbors. We become something like slaves of The Great They. This reliance on others, of course, is totally at odds with Required Masculinity's demand that you and I be independent and rely on no one.

A second significant consequence of your kowtow to The Great They is that a request from Them must be satisfied before your own desires, knowledge, or needs. It's Their "must", "should", and "ought." "You've got to go to Chicago this weekend." "The lawn needs mowing." "Get this proposal together by tomorrow at 9." "Don't be selfish. I need this done." "Vacation by yourself? You hate your family, don't you?" All a long list of demands and orders you've dutifully, if angrily, satisfied for years. And, you get only whatever bits of time and energy are left over from Their plans.

<u>Reduces considerably the attention paid to community and social considerations.</u> Required Masculinity has limited interests. Mostly it's money, power, and status with a lot of Dominance Competition, display, conformity, sex, and control thrown in. Beyond these, it has few if any interests. However, there are a lot of valuable things beyond these: community, welfare of others, environment, education, jobs for ordinary people, public health, effective government, family members, the arts, craftspeople, service providers and things like animals, inventions, the world, and real solutions. To the extent that Required Masculinity men pay attention to any of these, they use them for little more than showing to the world their power, wealth, and control. This masculinity and The Great They get away with this myopic view of life and the world because none of these community people or forces challenges the power and control The Great They grab. The only way any of these "little things" are able to stop Required Masculinity or The Great They is to throw a really big tantrum, e.g., earthquake, tsunami, epidemic, revolution, suicide bomb, climate change, economic depression, or financial collapse.

<u>Lacks ethical values.</u> Required Masculinity says that, to be a Man, I must use power, exercise control, make money, have sex with women, and be totally independent. It says nothing about ethics or values, which delivers a strong message that neither ethics nor values should be a part of a my life as a man. It is all "ends", and "any means is OK". Not caring about means, of course, leads me to not care about consequences. Dare I point to the Enron debacle, drug abuse in sports, graft and bribery in government, hidden product dangers, the war in Iraq, the VW pollution debacle, and purchased politics? If I dare to raise questions of ethics or values, this masculinity responds, "We're here to win. Be a Man. Stop whining."

For this masculinity, the only questions of right, wrong, good, and bad are whether I am exercising enough control, earning or getting enough money, or having enough sex to be a Man. Possessing the totems of this masculinity is right. Period. Nothing else should be considered. Any absence of its elements is bad. If ignoring any of these totems gains me health, intimacy, wisdom, creativity, spirituality, or personal satisfaction? The loss is bad, and the good for me is irrelevant.

<u>Excludes many needed skills, attitudes, and goals.</u> Once, I sat down and made a list of what Required Masculinity excludes from its world. I never could finish it; I was always finding something to add. The big ones: emotional literacy, compassion for others, public service, craftsmanship, knowledge. The medium sized ones: making sure that I have time for my kids and friends, making and being friends, taking that trip, playing that round of golf. The little ones: stopping to enjoy a sunset, playing a sex game my partner likes. In fact, for most of us, much of what makes life worth getting up for is excluded from this masculinity.

One of the biggest issues Required Masculinity excludes and prevents, a fact it carefully hides, is personal responsibility. Admittedly, for some people, this may be Required Masculinity's most attractive piece. Realistically, however, taking personal responsibility is essential for individual, community, and national survival and prosperity. This masculinity doesn't expressly ban personal responsibility for Men as obviously as it bans wearing dresses, but it gives me the perfect alibi: "I was only doing what a Man's supposed to do." And, of course, The Great They, who cheer my Required Masculinity, accept my failures without a murmur, as long as I "act like a Man". By eliminating real world personal responsibility, this masculinity leaves all of us with few ways to solve the problems this masculinity and The Great They system create and the damages they cause. Have you ever tried to get either of them to take responsibility for anything? When I do try to take personal responsibility seriously and challenge the messes They make, Required Masculinity and The Great They, of course, sneer and put me down as a "bleeding heart", and wimpy "do-gooder".

Discriminates against men who express masculinity in other ways. For men fully committed to Required Masculinity, only Men similarly committed are usually trusted, supported, seriously listened to, or respected. The second you're seen as "not much of a Man", you're sidelined with the women, children, and general nobodies. Often this takes the form of ignoring your ideas, contributions, and facts or overriding them with propaganda lectures, slogans, or extreme exercises of control and power. The tantrums a lot of political people throw at facts these days often sound very much like this discrimination in action.

Creates bigotry. Bigotry is the obstinate and blind attachment to an opinion that leads to excessive prejudice and intolerance, harm, and probably to stupidity. This sounds a lot like Required Masculinity, doesn't it? Males, The Great They, and our culture have adopted and defended this masculinity obstinately and blindly. It must not be challenged or disobeyed, and certainly not questioned. No exception must be allowed. It punishes each of us who doesn't conform to its "Truth", and refuses even to acknowledge an individual's positive qualities, let alone respects him. "You're no Man. You're a mouse." This bigotry does not stop with opinions and judgments. It regularly becomes action directed against you and me as if we were 12th century heretics ready for the stake.

If you continue to have doubts about the costs of Required Masculinity, I recommend reading *Self-Made Man* by Norah Vincent. Ms. Vincent disguised herself as a man for about eighteen months and hid herself in the male world. Her very direct and sometimes pungent comments offer you a street-smart view of men and the pressures we contend with to be male. The book is written in more or less chronological order, so the beginning has fewer really clear reactions and findings. Keep reading. Her experiences and observations are well worth your time and attention, and they make concrete much of what we have talked about here in abstract terms.

Cultural Pressures

We men are surrounded by people, institutions, and culture machines wielding a whole range of teaching, reward, and punishment schemes to encourage and force us Males into the Tools and Intentions of Required Masculinity. These forces include The Great They, its primary enforcement mechanism, and the vast media tools They control and manipulate. So effective are these efforts and so rigorously does The Great They apply them that "encourage" is insignificant in comparison to "required" and "forced". In short, Required Masculinity functions the same way that water does for our fish: obedience is the only option, or so The Great They announce in big, constantly repeating letters.

Like any other cultural concept, Required Masculinity is taught. Unlike other cultural concepts, however, Required Masculinity is taught and enforced incessantly and very intentionally, as the only view of masculinity. No one, of course, ever acknowledges that's what they're doing. It is as natural to us men as swimming is to our fish, and as omnipresent as the water he lives in. The expectations and rules of Required Masculinity are taught to us by our mothers when we're still in our cribs. They are taught to us by our fathers when they play with us. They are often brutally taught to us by our playmates, female and male. The older we get, the more people teach and enforce this masculinity on us. Our girlfriends and wives evaluate us on the basis of these expectations. Our employers propagandize and blatantly bribe us to meet these expectations. Our buddies and neighbors bully us into being this kind of man. Our churches and organizations demand we live by this masculinity for the sake of our souls. Our government almost always views every one of us as this kind of man and legislates, regulates, and judges based on the terms of this masculinity.

It is taught as simply as leaving the boy baby to cry longer than the girl baby before being picked up and attended to (statistically true apparently). One of the first phrases boys are likely to hear is, "Boys don't cry." Boys are told to take what they want, don't get pushed around, and win. If direct words are not effective enough, rules, requirements, policies, choices, and publicity will do it indirectly. Advertising messages, mostly subliminal but still very clear. Fiction. TV and movies. Women's choices of men to praise and marry. Articles and ads in men's and women's magazines. TV news choices about who gets the ten minutes of fame and for what. Corporate policies, procedures, expectations, and work demands. These all push the Tools and Intentions of Required Masculinity at us and leave us with no other choice. The next time you watch TV, or go to the movies, or thumb through a magazine, or read a bestseller say out loud what it tells you about men and masculinity. At least eighty percent of the time, I'll bet, this will be a pro-Required Masculinity message.

Rewards teach this masculinity. The boy who meets, or at least eagerly strives to meet, the rules and expectations of this masculinity becomes the popular boy, the boy most quickly chosen for a team or a group. He is the most eagerly sought out and encouraged by the girls and later by the women, i. e., he gets the most sex with women. This boy becomes the Man who gets promoted, gets the corner office, gets the CEO slot, becomes the celebrity, and Governor of the state.

Punishments teach this masculinity. These come as condemnations: "Only homos do that". They come as humiliation. "Sissy, wimp", "He's not Man enough," and "He's not a real Man" pour over the man who chooses not to meet, or cannot meet, the terms of Required Masculinity. They come as denials: he finds himself chosen last for the team or rejected, girls and women laugh at him and refuse to be seen with him, or jobs are not given when the person deciding on the hire or promotion announces, "He's not Man enough for the job." A politician is pronounced weak the minute he falters on this masculinity scale, and many recent political campaigns seem to be more about making Required Masculinity claims and defending this kind of manhood than about the public issues and the common good. Wives complain when their husbands can't tough it out on the job or stand up to some neighborhood bully. Even the kids get in the act, "My Dad can whip your Dad." "No, he can't." People do it with silence and indifference to the ideas coming from you when they judge you "not Manly". They do it by rarely praising the boys and men who express their own choices in their lives, choices that don't match this masculinity. The intellectual, creative, or compassionate man rarely gets elected or chosen for the job because "He's not a Man". The idea that respects rather than dominates people usually doesn't get on the agenda, or even put on the table sometimes.

All of these messages interconnect and reinforce each other, weaving such a tight thicket of Required Masculinity propaganda and enforcement that any other form of maleness has little chance in our culture. Like racism, sexism, and homophobia, the Required Masculinity message is pervasive and rooted deeply everywhere around us. The result is a 24/7, 360 degree, blare of messages that this masculinity is the only way a male can "be a Man".

Like all education processes, the most effective brainwashing for this masculinity occurs when men are young, as young as birth. This brainwashing seriously starts when a boy is about five, is very blatant until about 25, then very gradually fades into mostly indirect, but still very effective, reminders until he's in his sixties (when he can't possibly be counted "a Man" any more). The research and books of William Pollack and Michael Gurian look into the lives of boys and show the impact of this masculinity teaching on them. Before five years of age, boys develop mostly below the Required Masculinity radar and live their own natural lives. Then, teachers and other enforcers start shoving boys into Required Masculinity, and boys start experiencing heavy stress, anger, and confusion. Pollack and Gurian describe the damage this often causes to the boys. Men, stop and think about the stresses, humiliations, and sacrifices you lived through between six and eighteen – the friends you abandoned or lost, the fun you gave up, the things you "had to do" that you didn't like, the hopes you cut out – all in your effort to meet the demands Required Masculinity and The Great They were making on you.

bell hooks, a leading feminist writer, in her book *The Will to Change* presents the most damning picture I read anywhere of how we treat our boys. In homes driven by this masculinity, she claims, boys are regularly being seriously emotionally damaged. Parents do not teach or allow boys to learn to express their own feelings, to acknowledge that they have feelings, or even to find words for their emotions. If the fathers do not use physical violence to keep their sons in check, they use various techniques of psychological terrorism – shaming, tyrannical orders, degradation, and isolation. Mothers who don't abuse their sons directly do it indirectly by standing by and accepting their sons' indoctrination into Required Masculinity at the hands of fathers and other men. Single mothers regularly create a world of maternal sadism for their sons by coercing their sons to conform to the rules and expectations of "ordinary masculinity", i.e., Required Masculinity. The most insidious form of this tyranny, of course, always comes with a sweet parental smile, that look, and a nice pat on the back. The result, hooks says, are boys who act out or implode in their struggle to comply with the ceaseless demands that they act contrary, or at least in disregard of, their own natural feelings, choices, and understandings. This poisonous pedagogy of male power and male domination quickly frames the boy's notions of life and of being male. The young man easily ends up concluding that there is no possibility for him as he is and that, since he is not worthy in his natural form, he'd better find out how to be someone who is not him if he wants to be loved and accepted.

hook's picture is extreme, I agree. However, when I compare vague memories of myself at four with the somewhat less vague memories of myself at twelve, I can't completely reject hook's conclusions as wild-eyed rhetoric. Can you? Really? Most of us males, along about age six diligently started locking down and tearing out or deeply hiding everything in us that didn't fit the demands of Required Masculinity. Remember the joys and personal desires you gave up? By late teens I had swallowed the claim hook, line, and sinker that this masculinity was the only real world for us, though I was already skeptical about the value of its promised rewards.

Learning Required Masculinity is not like learning the multiplication tables in third grade: once we had the multiplication tables, these lessons stopped. The teaching of this masculinity is everywhere in our culture and goes on in every day of our lives. We never escape it, literally. If your boss doesn't do it, your wife will. If your buddies don't do it, almost every movie and TV program you watch will. No matter how well rewarded any man is for expressing this masculinity now, he knows that he is never a Man for life. He can fall off that sacred pedestal at any moment, often for just the appearance of not being not fully into this masculinity. Working to stay on this pedestal is our constant focus.

To preserve our public status as a Man, we have taught ourselves to always watch the people around us, especially The Great They who give the rewards or punishments. We feel forced to change our own opinions and actions to insure that The Great They judge us to be "a real Man." This boils down to choosing what They approve, doing what They approve, saying what They approve. It's the only way to make sure that we're always accepted as a Man and welcomed into The Great They that claims the world. The result of all of this over-the-shoulder paranoia is that we enforce this masculinity on ourselves by habit and manufactured need, which are the most effective enforcement tools of all.

> "Culture is thus not just a matter of language and naming. It is the medium by which individual perceptions and emotions find public voices, and the way those public voices shape the attitude of individuals towards themselves. In other words, we have two bodies: one that is our own, and another that belongs to the world in which we live ... interpenetrating aspects of each other ..." Braudy, *From Chivalry to Terrorism*, 176

Does this training system sound like bullying and bribery to you? It does to me. It's all about "Do this my way, and I'll give you money and power and tell the world you're a real Man. Do this some other way, and I'll yell to the world you're not a Man. You're a wimp, a fag, a little girl". Thanks to the propaganda power of Required Masculinity, we knuckle under to this bribery and bullying because we feel we have no choice.

What the benefits of this system are for the bribers and intimidators, however, aren't very clear. Obviously, if a man courageously saves my life, I benefit. But, what real benefit do I get from dominating some male or shooting down some man's project at work just to show my control? Maybe I benefit from a man who works the long hours I set for my factory and doesn't get paid much, but do I benefit from a man who has a big sex life? The strangest piece of this puzzle is the silence of the people who are actively harmed by men living Required Masculinity: the women, who are more likely to be harmed than benefited by being around these men; other men, who have a high probability of being dominated or even killed one way or another by these men; the boys seduced into Required Masculinity behavior against their personal choices; a son who lives under an authoritarian father.

School bullying has become especially public in the last thirty years from first grade through graduate school. Jessie Klein in *The Bully Society: School Shootings and the Crisis of Bullying in America's Schools* (2012) presents this issue at length. Her interviews with students, particularly middle-school and high-school students, show American schools as abettors in imposing "masculinity imperatives" (Required Masculinity in our terms) by bullying. She identifies this as one of the three bullying traits, along with "gender policing" and "normalized bullying". Her research into the motives of school shooters makes the point again and again that the shooters see shooting as the ultimate proof of their masculinity. The line between bullying and violence often fades as these males pump up their Required Masculinity commitments. All of this shows up in students and teachers in classrooms; in coaches, parents, and fans on athletic fields; and administrators and teachers in faculty meetings. Late in her book, Klein looks at workplace shootings. She finds the same social culture as she found in the schools, although not quite so blatant. Although these shootings can be disregarded as so much revenge, Klein points again to the shooter's beliefs that his manhood had been questioned and shooting proved his Manliness.

Another significant source of Required Masculinity's power may rest to some degree not in something that is but in something that isn't. The transition from child to adult for women, menstruation, is biological, obvious, and inescapable for them. In its wake comes a number of important physical and psychological changes that the female is forced to adjust to and cope with. Boys experience nothing this disruptive and inescapable in their puberty transition. Pubic and facial hair? Once we take pride in it, we ignore it or handle it without thought. Hard-ons, sex, and jacking off? We enjoy the moments of fun and pleasure, but then go on with whatever we were doing.

Traditional cultures, however, take and took a totally different view of this transition of boys to men. Almost all of them had very substantial "initiation" rites in which the men of the community led and pushed boys through a carefully planned order of rituals and activities. These covered a wide range of things, e.g., community history and laws, local myths, physical cutting and marking, wilderness isolation, and in some places an organized first copulation experience. This transition experience in any serious form has been absent for European and American boys for probably a thousand years plus. I suspect that the effect of this loss was tempered a bit by the fact that for centuries boys transitioned to manhood with their father beside them, as a model of adult male, as they daily worked together in family fields and shops. When the Industrial Revolution came along, most fathers went off to the factory or the city, and the boys lost their on-site mentors and models. Then, they were separated even further by being sent off to a school. Today's classrooms, of course, are almost always run by a female not a male. Now, they almost never have a mature male as a daily model of manhood.

Think back to your years 11-18. How much education in being a man did you get from a male over thirty-five, even your father? For the better part of the last hundred years, boys got most of their training from two sources: their peers and the entertainment world. Their peers know almost nothing about being a mature male, except the Required Masculinity propaganda. Okay, the sex education is often handled really pretty effectively by peers. But, as you know now, sex is only a small part of being a mature male. The entertainment world pushes the Required Masculinity male as the hero, the god, and the real Man. With all of this landing on us eager, impressionable boys, can it be a surprise that we usually think sexual and physical dominance and money are the signs of being a Man and so chase these goals? Who do we have around us to lead us or push us into broader and deeper understanding of what a man we can be?

Strangely enough, however, some men do become fully developed, mature men despite the propaganda and expectations of the Required Masculinity awash in our culture. It is a mystery to me how this happens and where the crucial touchstones for this are. I suspect that the experience of finding a fulfilling activity, real love, and a family of our own play huge roles in the steps we finally take to step away from Required Masculinity. One interesting note in passing: in recent years, as these three probable touchstones have drifted later and later in the lives of males, late twenty and thirty year old males seem to function these days more like college sophomores than mature men. Michael Kimmel in his book *Guyland* discusses this rising phenomenon and it impacts.

CHALLENGE #2: GETTING AWAY FROM REQUIRED MASCULINITY

Step One is to break the hold of Required Masculinity, to actually see the Required Masculinity grip and to understand it. This book is trying very hard to make sure that you can do both of these. Whether you choose to see or understand is your decision, of course.

Step Two is to decide whether you're going to ignore what you see and understand and go on living in Required Masculinity or to face up to this and break its hold. Given the immense power of Required Masculinity, to break its hold on you can't possibly mean defeating it on a cultural scale. You and I can, however, defeat it on our own levels, in our personal lives, by choosing and expressing our chosen masculinity Tools and Intentions. Although I can't change the vast public society in which I exist, I can move from one section of this public society to a more compatible one. E.g., I can move to a gay neighborhood if I'm gay, move to an evangelistic church from a Catholic church, or move to an arts neighborhood from a country club neighborhood. You can find a job that stokes your interests and desires instead of dragging yourself along in a rut you hate. You can choose new friends and leave the Required Masculinity types to their grim little box. You can party or play your sport in a setting less awash with Required Masculinity than the one you party or sport in now.

Step Three is to carry out constantly and consistently whatever you decide in Step Two. Carrying out a decision to stay in Required Masculinity will be very easy, just go on as you have for years and work a little harder at ignoring your internal disagreements with its expectations and demands. Carrying out a decision to break away from this and going your own way will need a lot of determination, persistence, and change. Basics on how to do this are found throughout these eight Challenges.

How Do I Get Away From Required Masculinity At Work?

For most men, work is the primary enforcer of Required Masculinity. It's built on money, power and obedience, Dominance Competition, and control, and its Tools are money, power, dominance, and control. With cellphones, texting, and email in its claws, it consumes almost every waking second of our time. However, men have found several available roads out of this masculinity at work.

One way is to find an ally. Any fight is better with someone on your side. If your ally is also a guy with authority or influence in your workplace, so much the better. The more allies, the more protected you all are. What does an ally in this situation look like? A guy who respects a man's personal choice. A guy who also operates against the Required Masculinity grain. A guy who respects and uses some special skill or knowledge that you bring to your job. A guy whose actions you respect and support. Who this ally is, of course, depends on all of the factors you see in your particular work situation.

Finding him is the challenge. Here are some possible options to improve your hunt. Put your positions and priorities out loud and clear, and let them draw him to you, though this could mean high risk for you. Don't assume that every man at work is gung-ho Required Masculinity; listen and watch carefully. Sooner or later you'll see a man roll his eyes at some Required Masculinity statement or hear him speak, or more likely act, against one. When the risk of punishment is low (e.g., in the cafeteria, not a department meeting), let others know the way you'd really like so see things managed. In a private meeting with your supervisor, offer your ideas and requests. Your allies are out there; it's a matter of singing your song at a listening moment and being patient and alert.

A second way to get away from Required Masculinity is to play its game only at work. How comfortable are you riding two horses going in different directions at the same time? It's not easy, but it can be done. However, it carries considerable risk that Required Masculinity will win just because you play its game more hours per week than you play your Personal Masculinity game. You need to be very self-disciplined to do this two-horse ride successfully. Figuring out some trigger that will effectively shift your head from Required Masculinity to your Personal Masculinity at the right moment and from your Personal Masculinity to Required Masculinity at that right moment will help you a lot. Maybe this trigger is some word to say out loud or some quirky gesture that reminds you of which environment you're in. Maybe there is some mental or verbal game you can play that will get you, your brain, and your emotions to switch from work to your own life.

A third way exists if you have some leadership role at work. You have golden opportunities on this issue. Using your authority and influence, you can build a group, office, or even a department that suppresses some or much of the control and Dominance Competition of Required Masculinity and gives freedom to the personal Tools and Intentions of your staff. Try putting yourself in an odd location at the meeting table or backing one of your employees against the powers that be when you're comfortable with your employee's suggestion. Conduct your meetings from the Personal Masculinity perspective: listen more to the facts than to the "oughts", put the different idea on the agenda, give the quiet ones some developmental time. Keep asking for options when the usual options are all on the table. Use your performance reviews to encourage the employee's ideas or ask what she needs to make her best contributions and give it to her. Building this kind of work environment creates several benefits. You get to work in an environment closer to the one you want. You are also likely to get more interesting ideas and more creative solutions from your staff. And, you create a working model that shows the rest of your company that the Tools and Intentions of Personal Masculinities are a good way to manage men and improve your company's accomplishments.

The ultimate way to escape Required Masculinity at work is to quit the job and find an operation in which Required Masculinity is less powerful or, best yet, where Personal Masculinity operates freely. Yes, there are such places, lots of them. The trick is to find them when you can see a potential company only from the outside. A useful rule of thumb might be to figure out if the company's dominant goal is money or if it has other goals as well. If the dominant goal is just money, it will probably be driven by Required Masculinity. If there is something more than money or money is just at the "We need to pay our bills" level, the company will probably be open to other kinds of masculinity. Large institutions and organizations usually have strong financial goals and will tend towards the Required Masculinity side. Your best option may be with a medium to small organization or one in which you personally know the masculinity attitudes of the bosses. Hi-tech businesses seem to expend a lot of money and publicity convincing potential employees that they don't operate in the Required Masculinity mode. However, their obsession with money, market control, and competition leads me to question their claims. Since I never worked in one of these, I cannot judge. But, if I were the right age to work in one, I would walk in very cautiously.

The gutsiest way to go is to stand up to the tigers and demonstrate to them what Personal Masculinity can get for them and their company. This will be the toughest option to carry out but, if you really like the work you're doing or the mission of your company, you might want to try it. Then, the question is: How are you going to do this? At a minimum, you are going to have to find a way for your Personal Masculinity to show your fellow workers and the big boss what this can bring to them. To do this, you will need to be alert to opportunities as they appear. Two dangers here can catch you: saying "No, do it my way", and creating an all-out battle. To your co-workers, both of these can sound just like Required Masculinity Dominance Competition and trigger a full-scale Required Masculinity response. Obviously, this is not what you want. You can probably slide around these dangers by using a "what about this?" approach or a "wouldn't it be easier (more productive, etc.), if …" approach.

Am I Stuck With Required Masculinity?

Unlike a fish in his bowl, you are not stuck with the Required Masculinity environment, however much Required Masculinity propaganda and the people around you insist that you are. Take off the Required Masculinity glasses you've been wearing for years. Really look around you at the men you know, particularly at a man you admire. Does he always act according to this masculinity, on every issue? Does he always chase the next sexual conquest? Does he always seek to dominate every relationship he's in? Is winning all he thinks about? Does he always walk independently of everyone? Unless you move among a very unusual group of men, you will find that the men you admire choose other than Required Masculinity often, very often, maybe more often than they act in accordance with it.

They can show you that omnipotent Required Masculinity can be ignored and rejected and how to do both.

If there is one clear message in this book, I hope that it is that you can walk away from Required Masculinity and survive. Challenges #3-#8 are filled with ways to do this and strong encouragements to use them.

What If I Can't Leave Required Masculinity?

Is it "can't"? Or, is it "don't really want to"? Are these "can't" and "don't want to" reasons so controlling of your actions and thoughts that you literally cannot make any other choice? What gives them this control over you? Why are these reasons so persuasive with you? Your freedom and a more satisfying life may depend on you looking very hard at these reasons. Parental or spousal expectations often have enormous control over you and make any other choices seem impossible, but these are not laws. Despite Required Masculinity's preaching that it is rock solid, this apple can easily be divided, and you can pick and choose the parts that work for you and leave the rest. Many of the men you know have probably done just this in varying degrees from time to time, even the most Required Masculinity committed man you know. Don't forget to remember that whatever you choose today you can always unchoose tomorrow.

I Don't Really Want To.

Some men don't see Required Masculinity as confining. They find meaning and fulfillment in the rewards, money, power, sex opportunities, and status offered by this masculinity. Or, even if it does confine them in some ways, these are minor matters in comparison to the rewards Required Masculinity gives them. When deep in the satisfaction of these rewards and the present, however, it is easy to ignore how the instability of these rewards creates some of dark side circles.

This instability shows up in a number of very ordinary circumstances for most men: he loses his job, his wife leaves him, a manlier man moves into the office, he gets called "wimp" in an office confrontation, his child attacks him for something he's doing that the child doesn't agree with, he doesn't get a promotion. With this, he loses some or all of his status as a Man and finds his confidence and belief in himself faded or vanished. This instability also shows up in his forties or fifties when many men committed to Required Masculinity begin to seriously question the satisfactions they get from money, power, sex, and Dominance Competition. We know this as "mid-life crisis".

The goodies that Required Masculinity claims to deliver can be very seductive, particular when you've swallowed its propaganda for years. If this is the choice you want, and I emphasize "choice" and "want", to live with, almost no one will criticize you. When you choose to remain with this masculinity, of course, you won't get just the benefits. You'll also get this instability and the impacts we discussed back in Challenge #1. You can't escape these, so you'll need to figure out how you are going to deal with them. If you stick with only a couple of the elements of this Required Masculinity, the costs will probably be fewer, but you will still face some of them. The more of Required Masculinity you take, the more of the costs you will have to cope with. If these costs begin to look big and ugly to you, go back and reconsider the reasons why you choose to stay with this masculinity and how much of it you really want to stay committed to. Always, you can walk away from it and find your own masculinity Tools and Intentions. I did it at sixty.

I Can't Leave.

Why "can't"? The Required Masculinity propaganda and its enforcers are too strong for you? Your brain configuration absolutely fits this masculinity? Is it that you just don't want to leave? If you think the enforcers are too strong for you, think again. Much of this book is about a man's ability to leave Required Masculinity and ways to do it. Many men, myself included, can attest to being able to leave this masculinity and build much more satisfying lives with our Personal Masculinities. In evaluating the strength of Required Masculinity, don't forget all the things you don't like about yourself in Required Masculinity mode. This dislike is probably stronger and more dependable than Required Masculinity.

If you think your brain configuration has control of the issue, please review this issue on page 24. Your brain is not structured just for this masculinity; it's just that your other brain functions are under-developed. You can grow and expand these other functions. You can also reduce the strength of the Required Masculinity brain functions by reducing or eliminating your use of them.

What is persuading you to stay with Required Masculinity?

- Fear of the usual "you're not a Man" attacks from family, friends, and business colleagues if you leave Required Masculinity and follow your personal masculinity?

- Fear that, if you leave Required Masculinity, you won't know how to live as a male, how to decide what to think or how to act as one?

- Lack of confidence that any alternative to Required Masculinity will give you a satisfying life? In other words, the risk of the change is just too big?

- You like the benefits you get from living Required Masculinity and don't want to lose them?

- A few elements of Required Masculinity fit you very comfortably?

- Finding and living a Personal Masculinity looks just too hard or scary to do?

Only you can evaluate the strength and persuasiveness of each of these reasons for you. In this evaluation, however, please keep a couple of thoughts in mind. Fear is rarely a good basis for decisions, as I'm sure you've discovered more than once in your life. How often has taking the easy way out gotten you real progress or a real solution? Your goal here is to find a way to be male that fits comfortably with the real you, with what you want to do and be, with the truths you understand and want to live by for the rest of your life.

CHALLENGE #3:
FINDING MY REAL SELF

A Self-based man differs from Required Masculinity in three fundamental ways. First, a Self man is a matter of his choice, your choice; Required Masculinity is a matter of culturally forced compliance. Second, a Self man expresses himself uniquely; Required Masculinity demands conformity to uniform thoughts, goals, and actions. Third, a Self man comes from within the man himself; Required Masculinity is imposed from the outside by external sources.

Many men, myself included, have settled into this Self-based life because we feel at ease, very secure, and satisfied here. It's like the swing that, before you strike the ball, tells you it's a home run. Kids have a lot of this sense of personal certainty, and we get to feel this a bit when they throw their arms around us in their sheer exuberance of living. When I and many other men moved from Required Masculinity to our Self-based, natural life, this kind of energy and experience came back into our lives. We are free of the grinding tension that comes from always worry about whether we're "being a Man". Our lives fill with the passion, energy, and joy that hug us and fill our minds and hearts with the certainty that this is what our life is supposed to be for us. An unexpected benefit of this change for me has been that I've become more helpful and kinder to others than I ever was as a man living by Required Masculinity. Also, when you go to your Self for your maleness, you get a custom fit maleness, and a flexible maleness. This makes you more comfortable, responsive, and stable. Oh, we don't get our way all the time; pervasive Required Masculinity and other Selfs regularly contest this. But, the game isn't rigged against us anymore.

Many people will tell you that leaving Required Masculinity and building a Self-based, natural life is selfish. This life is selfish from The Great They point of view, since you are no longer giving Them what They want just because They want it. On the other hand, a Self-based life is not all you and no them; it fits others into your Tools and your Intentions. Instead of grabbing everything from others for me, I actually know that I need only the few pieces that really fit my Self and only enough of those as I actually need. I can easily respect and support other people's needs without feeling I'm losing something.

At this stage, your Self is probably vague to you. This is not a surprise, since Required Masculinity keeps most men from getting to know their Selfs. When we were boys, though, we knew our feelings, what ifs, choices, and abilities, all of which reflected our natural Selfs. In spite of how tightly we locked down as teenagers to climb into Required Masculinity, these boy things continue to show up now and then, don't they? They often come at inappropriate times and in ways you can't control – as opposition to something everyone else okays, a dislike for no apparent reason, a fit of emotional lock-up on the way home from work, stealing a box of your favorite cookies while shopping, anger "over nothing", your emotion-laden response to an innocent question, wakefulness in the middle of the night, that drive into the middle of nowhere for no reason you can think of, taking an extra helping of your favorite food on the rare times it shows up even though you aren't hungry. These are each the voice of your Self wriggling loose and shouting, "Here I am".

For many men, the Self-based life has one huge negative. It is not a pre-fab, ready-to-go, off-the-shelf product. Each man has to do his own Self investigation and create his own Self profile. Even for men who have done their investigation or are willing to do it, a Self-based life still can look hard and scary. You have to push yourself at the beginning to express the Tools and Intentions that are your particular Self and to stand up for them in the face of all the punishments that Required Masculinity and The Great They will throw at you for a while. These are legitimate worries and will trip you up from time to time, as they did all of us who have walked this path. However, they are not un-climbable obstacles, and certainly not bolted doors. We all learned to maneuver through them soon, and so can you.

Finding one's own Self man can feel impossible. When I started on this hunt for myself, I wondered if anything were in me to find and, even if it existed, I doubted that I could find any of it. As my early stumbling discoveries about my Self turned up, these doubts faded, and I increased my discovery rate. At one point, when I was really irritated about how long my learning process was taking, an insight hit me. It took all the machinations of the highly effective Required Masculinity and The Great They systems working on me from birth to age twenty-five to lock me into Required Masculinity manhood and a constant re-enforcement for the next twenty-five years to keep me loyal to it. Seen from this fifty-year perspective, my five years of concentrated efforts that led me away from Required Masculinity to my Self looked almost miraculously short.

Finding a process to use and a support system to lean on will be an enormous help. The Self-Investigation process I am going to outline in the rest of this Challenge will provide this process for you. This is exactly what its name says, Self investigation. You dig into yourself to find out who you actually are and to select your masculinity Tools and Intentions to express who you are. I discovered, or maybe "pasted together" is a better description, this process over several years of scratching and scrabbling for a new way for me to be more comfortable and expressive and be a man. I gradually nailed down the unique perspectives, desires, wisdoms, fears, and concerns that were who I was. I call this person my Self man. When I had accumulated pages of these answers, I organized them into a Self Profile. Support for these efforts you can easily find in a men's group and a Men's Weekend. The openness and caring of the men in these groups encouraged me to step out of Required Masculinity on my own terms and carried me – okay, sometimes pushed me – through my endless questions for several more years. In the men's groups I have facilitated, I have seen this same escape happen time and again. If these aren't available for you, I hope that you find a partner, friend, or therapist who will support your search and encourage you.

What Things Are Really Who I Am?

We all know the proverbial test for good art: "You'll know it when you see it." The test for knowing your Self is similar: you'll know your Self when you feel it. Yes, "feel", that word men don't like. Even before I began doubting Required Masculinity, I knew that my feelings gave me truer information about myself than any philosophy or rule being thrown at me. Oh, I ignored or rejected what my feelings said, as a good Required Masculine male should of course, but I couldn't say, "They're wrong". Whatever resonates with joy or calm at your innermost place of being is part of your Self. I have no idea what any of the pieces of your Self will look like; those are your discoveries, and they may surprise you. However, I'm almost certain that your Self will, like mine, be a kaleidoscope of profound truths and the most ephemeral of sensations: peanut butter and banana sandwiches and integrity, walking in blizzards and textile creativity. You're looking for ALL of these pieces, big, little, universal, and trite.

At its most simple, your Self is that voice in you that says No when Required Masculinity and They say Yes. It is the unique combination of desires, perspectives, capacities, feelings, fears, and goals that make up your particular person and describe your particular abilities and potentials. At its most complex, it is that bundle of things in you that feels solid, stable, true, strong, and reliable within yourself.

Of every idea, feeling, perspective, action that proposes itself as a part of your Self ask these questions:

- Am I, at the innermost place of my being, joyful and calm over this idea, action, goal?

- Do I want to stand by this, live this? Not just *willing* to stand by it, but *wanting* to stand by it, and the wanting is the important piece.

- Would I get enjoyment and satisfaction out of living this every day? Not can I *tolerate* it here and there, but will I *choose* it whenever I can.

When you get a Yes on all three questions for a proposed piece of your Self, you have definitely found a piece. If you get two Yeses, you have probably found a piece of your Self, but you might want to test this piece a bit before accepting it totally. If you get just one Yes, it's probably not a piece of your Self, although it might worth thinking about some more. If you get no Yeses, the thing is definitely not part of your Self.

How Do I Find This Self Man Of Mine?

Don't let your ignorance or inexperience of your Self stop you from searching for the pieces of who you are. I found that my Self was ready and eager to teach me who I was; all I had to do was ask real questions and really hear and accept what it told me. It took me a while to get this hearing and accepting thing going, since I'd spent most of fifty years blocking it out and Required Masculinity or The Great They were still trying to cover up my Self's answers. Early on I used this crutch: if the idea were outrageous and would probably upset at least half the people close to me, I assumed that it was my Self talking and adopted it. If it sounded "right" or "ought to be", I assumed that it was Required Masculinity or The Great They talking and rejected it. After I'd identified a bunch of Self messages, of course, I began to learn the shape of my Self and could decide more rationally which messages to accept and which to reject. If the new message "fit" the Self messages I had already accepted, then I adopted the new one, even if I didn't have a clue at that moment as to what it meant. If it didn't fit? Chop, chop, and out it went. One of the very reassuring things I discovered along the way was that my Self messages are vastly more internally consistent, and more consistent with reality than the messages from Required Masculinity or The Great They ever were.

The practical core of the Self-Investigation option is the Investigation Sheet (see page 91). Here's how to use it. Begin by making a dozen or so copies of the Self Investigation Sheet. Or, you can just use it as a format to work on sheets of lined paper.

Step 1. Event. Find an event and write it in the Events column in a few words, just enough to jog your memory. This can be anything. In a few paragraphs I will suggest a variety of paths to follow to find useful Events. For the sake of understanding the process, let's assume that at the moment you are looking for things that make you uncomfortable. Every day, identify at least one event during that day when you felt really uncomfortable. Let's say that you really squirmed when you overheard a big argument in the hallway of your office in which one person was attacking another person verbally. Write down "hallway attack" in the Events column. The more Events you list, of course, or the longer you keep building this list the more Self information you will get to work with.

Step 2. Issue. Once a week or so – soon enough that you don't forget the details of any Event you wrote down – sit down with your list. Think about *what* made you uncomfortable about each Event, the issue in it that upset you. It could be a perspective, philosophy, sensual dislike, anything, whatever it was that bothered you. Be as specific and concrete as you can. The more specific and concrete you make this issue the more useful it becomes in finding a Self Factor. Write this down, again briefly but concretely, in the Issue column beside your Event. In our hallway attack example, let's say that what really bothered you was that you didn't like somebody judging another person on the basis of just the speaker's desires or assumptions. Write "judging by desires" on your Investigation Sheet as the Issue for your hallway Event.

Step 3. Self Factor. To get from Issue to Self Factor, you need to find what in your Self was feeling trapped, ignored, or harmed in the Issue. This may be what the Issue ignored, prevented, punished, or did not consider. This needs to be something positive and concrete, what you do like not what you don't like. Don't like is easy to find, but a life built on dislikes, hatreds, and fears is almost always depressing and unsatisfying. In your hallway Event, your Issue was the basis on which a person is to be judged. Maybe the Self Factor here might be your conviction that only facts should govern judgments. Write this down in the Factor column. The items in the Factor column are pieces of your Self. They need not be elegantly phrased or even very clearly phrased at first; some of mine were indecipherable for quite a while. Eventually, you will refine each Factor statement so that you understand it more clearly.

That's it, the process of the Investigation Sheet in three steps. It's a simple process mechanically, but not substantively. In each of these steps, keep everything as concrete and concise as possible. So, only rugged honesty works here. No "ditto" entries. Each Event and Issue has something unique to tell you, so find these unique words each time. This can be a pain in the head and the fingers, but I still find that the result is worth the effort every time.

The more paths you follow, the more Self Factors you'll find. It may be more effective if you use separate Investigation Sheets or sets of Investigation Sheets for each path you pursue. Here are some paths that have produced useful information for men in my groups and for myself and some hints for making each path work for you:

Things that make you uncomfortable. This can be anything that makes you uncomfortable, people, things, events, ideas, anything, or the absence of same. This path works best if you pick items that make you the most uncomfortable. Usually these are the clearest to you and the easiest for you to understand and reduce to concrete words.

Things that you dislike or hate. Finding the Self Factor for this kind of Event requires a mental game. Hate or dislike is a negative. Remember, you want to reach positive Self Factors in the end. The game here is to find the positive in the negative. Let's say that you think classical music is boring. I would suggest that your Self Factor might be that you like music that's got a lot of rhythm. Or, you dislike radio talk shows. After some thought, maybe your Self Factor here comes up as, "I want to listen to anger-free people" or "I want to listen to thinking people not emotional babblers".

In my experience, it is hardest to find the Factors in big negatives, those sweeping "I hate all ..." statements. Our emotion is often easier to identify than the Issue or Self Factors driving it. More than once, I had to accept that a Factor in an Event had nothing to do with what I thought I hated or disliked; it really was about something I associated with the Event, not the Event itself. For years and years I hated, really hated, athletics and anything to do with athletics and sports. I finally realized that what I really hated was the Domination Competition mindset that pervades athletics and the humiliation I lived through in school for my lack of athletic skills and competition drive. Once I pinned these down, I discovered that my Self Factors here were Testing Competition and respecting people in spite of what they can't do.

Two kinds of hates and dislikes can mislead your search for Self Factors: hatred of ideas and hatred of people. Our hate and dislike of an idea is often our dislike or hatred of the people we associate with that idea, the consequences we fear may come from that idea, or a judgment on ourselves that we cannot understand the idea. Your Issues in the hates lie somewhere in these items. Our hatred or dislike of a person is usually about the consequences he or she has created for us, and your Issue lies in those consequences. You'll be tempted to just blame the person or the idea. However, Self investigation is not about blame or responsibility; it's about finding in your Self what triggers your Issues and pulling out of this trigger the Self Factors that power it.

SELF INVESTIGATION SHEET

EVENT   ISSUE   SELF FACTOR

1.

2.

3.

4.

5.

6.

7.

Let's say you hate that bitch Carol W. at work. Why? Maybe it's because she gave you wrong information for an important project. So, isn't being given wrong information by a co-worker, not Carol personally, what you really hate? Your Self Factor here is probably wanting to operate on the basis of truth and honesty.

The quiet voice within. Each of us hears voices ... and we're not crazy. We hear the voices of parents, teachers, media, and institutions from our past pretty regularly. But, there has been one voice that is always clear and always points to what you know is true about yourself; maybe you call this your conscience, or your Elf. Whatever you name it, you've learned over the years that it speaks your truth in hard moments. When I was deep into my Self investigation, I realized that this voice was the most direct voice of my Self I had. If the statement of your voice is a positive statement or easy to understand, skip the Event and Issue steps and write the statement directly into the Self Factor column. If it's a negative statement or one that doesn't seem very clear to you, dig for the Issue behind it and then find its Factor.

Consistent behaviors. We each have behaviors, desires, attitudes that we consistently do over and over again. What do you always do when you've had a tough day to revive your spirits? Chocolate is my fix. When you have a long To Do List, what kinds of projects do you always do first? Mine always involve writing. All of these regular things may be pieces of your Self. Notice the "may"; this is a crucial word here. Consistency can be the result of the way we're built; it can also be the way we've trained ourselves or been trained. Trained behaviors, however, are highly unlikely to be pieces of your Self. In my experience, the most useful consistent behaviors are likely to be of two kinds: those I've done since my childhood, and those that I consistently choose when I have time to myself. Another likely source is the behavior you use to soothe yourself, soothe not anesthetize. These behaviors are Events. Skip the Issues, and find the Self Factors: what attracts you to these behaviors, what they satisfy, or the specific pleasure they give.

Favorite possessions. I am talking about the possessions that you've had for a very long time, particularly those you've hauled in and out of your homes and apartments for years. They can be little or big. I've hauled around a baby grand piano for years, including a crane delivery and removal through a third floor window with two inches to spare. How much insight does it take for you to decide that love of music is my Self Factor here? The possession is the Event, and why you keep it is the Issue. The Self Factor is the reason you keep it or the quality the item raises in you that makes you feel "at home" with it.

If you are a pack rat or have just lived in one place for a very long time, try this version instead: If I were moving into a one-room apartment, what out of this mess would I take with me?

What do I like to do with my time when it's my own? This is the old "Blue Sky" question therapists and vocational counselors love to ask us. "If you could do anything with your time (and money, training, and experience weren't issues), what would you do?" Or, what would you_rather be doing right now? Or, whom would you like to be with? Your answer is the Event. You can probably skip an Issue here. The Self Factor is the concrete benefit you think you get from the action you want.

Fears. With most of your family, friends, jobs, and the rest of our culture dedicated to enforcing the rules and expectations of Required Masculinity, we men are riddled with fears of punishment for being judged not a man, although we rarely admit these fears even to ourselves. These Required Masculinity-based fears do not tell you anything very useful about your Self, so don't bother with them.

The fears that are useful to investigate are fears of particular behaviors and events and fears of losing a particular person or thing. Especially useful to think about is fear of a behavior or thing that you have already experienced more than once. One-time fears may be more about surprise than fear. Most of us men belittle our fears. "This is silly." "Nobody else fears this." "A Man fears nothing." Don't step under this umbrella in your Self investigation. If you fear X, then X is your Event. Period.

Your Issue is why you fear, not what you fear. Your Self Factor here is something positive that is upset or offended by the Event. You get to this with the same mental game I described in the Things You Dislike path. You need to figure out what you want instead of the Issue you listed. If your Event is losing your job, maybe your Issue is you don't want to feel like a failure. Your Self Factor could be that you need explicit approvals in order to feel confident.

Body messages. The physical condition of our bodies can be a remarkable messenger, and one that men ignore almost universally. The usual drill applies here. The body message, usually distress or pleasure in some form, is the Event. Since the body message is always responsive, the Issue lies not in what triggered response, but in what your body finds so important that it reacts to it. Tom saw you punished and degraded by the boss one day. Now, every time Tom appears in your life, this triggers again the feelings you had during that scene. You'll find the Self Factor in your reaction to the punishment and degradation, not in Tom or what he did at the time. It is really important on this path to make everything as concrete and concise as possible.

Warning: your physical reaction may respond not to an event but to some personal connotation of that event. For example, your stomach goes into knots when you see Tom again. The Issue that your body is reacting to is that you're still furious at the way that former boss treated you six years ago, not to Tom who was only a witness to your event. Your Factor lies in why your body still reacts to the punishment scene.

Long-term stress will probably be hard for you to identify as a message to be investigated, since it may feel like your ordinary condition rather than something notable. An easier way to proceed on this may be to wait for a clear rise in this stress that you can identify and then use the cause of this rise for your Event. The longer that you have lived with the stress, the harder it will probably be to find the Issue and Self Factor here. Identifying when this stress began or when it was especially high, and searching that time may lead you to your Issue and Self Factor.

Other paths. Follow whatever questions present themselves to reach Events, Issues, and Factors. One Event might lead you to several Issues, or one Issue to several Self Factors. On more than one occasion in my Identification work, an apparently clear Self Factor morphed into something totally different when I accidentally thought of it in connection with another Issue or saw it from a new perspective. This Self investigation process works a lot like combing heavily snarled hair. At the beginning, you work out the easy snarls on the surface. As you keep combing, you work deeper and deeper, getting the snarls you missed the first, second, and third times. If you keep combing, you get to the really nasty snarls down deep, the ones you only feared might be there. Each combing straightens out a bit more, and you get the hair a little more organized and manageable. With Self investigation, each battery of questions brings new pieces of your Self to the surface for you to understand and express. If you stop asking questions, you stop getting answers and learn no more of who you are. Twenty years later, I still find myself occasionally in a Self-Investigation knot.

Scary Self Factor

First, don't drop the Sheet in the trash.

If you are absolutely honest with yourself during this Self investigation, you will almost certainly find some Factors that shock or stun you to your core; every man walking down this Self Investigation road has faced this. This moment is not easy, and it may take you a long time to accept this shocking Factor as truly part of who you are. Question it. Shake it as a puppy shakes a toy. Argue with it. Despise it. Shove it into a dark closet for a while. If your scary Factor stands up to your abuse and keeps knocking for your attention, you need to deal with it in the end.

This shocking Factor can be anything. It can come in any number of negative and positive guises: you really hate your family, pornography gives you a lot of pleasure, you can't stand your work, you loathe your family reunions and beer parties, you really like watching movies with lots of gruesome killings, you can't stand living in big cities when you've lived in them for your whole life, you'd really like to walk nude down Main Street. Whatever it is, if you consider the Factor a shock, shocking it is for you. Most likely, it is shocking only because you've never seen it as part of yourself before. Whether it is shocking good or shocking bad depends on lots of things in your life, most of which I can't even guess. The strong temptation will be to say it's bad, but that's mostly your shock, Required Masculinity, or The Great They talking. Get a grip on this temptation.

Let the idea sink in. Given the experience of other men and myself, I suspect that before too long you will finally admit that you've suspected for years something like this was part of you and you've stomped on it every time it raised its head. Then, start figuring out what you want to do with this Factor.

You can always say, "Okay, that's who I am, but I am not going to express that part of me right now." This is what the "closet" is about for gay men and transgendered people when they first discover who they are. It's a time out while you learn to accept and understand something surprising about yourself. You can, also, say, "Oh, shit. What am I going to do about this? Yeah, it's picked away at me for years. At thirty (or forty, or fifty-two, or whatever age you are), it's time to finally look this Factor straight in the eye and deal with it." This is what "coming out of the closet" is all about. I don't mean to imply by using this "closet" language here that you're going to discover that you are gay or really a woman. However you look at it, this moment of discovery isn't the Monday morning meeting at work. Absolutely nothing requires you to disclose this surprise to anyone. You are free to leave it "in the closet" for as long as you like. However, do not, I beg you, refuse to understand your shocking Factor or try to erase it. It won't go away, as I suspect you already know. It is a part of you. Better to know and accept the whole of yourself and not express a particular Factor than to be frightened of a part of yourself.

Coming to terms with whatever this shocking Factor is probably works best in three steps:

1. Accept that the Factor is really part of who you are and that you cannot escape it.

2. Understand the Factor. This can range from looking for its causes, for places and times to serious research its content and behavior, and for the options it can open for you.

3. Find ways to integrate what you learn into the rest of your life. Doing this quietly leads you out of "the closet" without having to make an announcement with trumpets and drums blaring.

This process may take you five minutes, or five months, or five years. Maybe you'll be eager, maybe you won't touch the thing for three years. Whatever your situation, you might find it helpful to talk to a close friend (if you are lucky enough to have one), to join a men's support group, to talk with a therapist, to find others who have seen this terrible Factor, to read stories about people living this Factor. In the end, the most important thing to remember is that what you do about this shocking Factor is your choice and nobody else's. You can accept and express this Factor to any degree you find yourself able to, and you can change this degree tomorrow and again next month, and again. You can let your acceptance and expression dawdle for as long as you wish or show this Factor only in certain places and to certain people. This is all *your* choice.

My surprise Factors were: I'm gay, and I'm a creative person, not heterosexual despite two marriages and three kids and not the hard-ass administrator or Chief Financial Officer that I played for years. Eventually, my last marriage ended, and I learned to express my gay nature, and I developed my creativity as artist and writer. I said many an "Oh, my God" during these changes, but I managed them and am happier now than I have ever been.

Will you have to make such immense changes? I can't begin to guess. Look around you, and I'll bet you can find lawyers who turned themselves into teachers, CEOs who turned themselves into farmers or resort owners, carpenters who became musicians, and retailers who became bankers or nurses. Who knows what pleasures you can bring yourself by honestly answering quiet questions about who you are.

Create Your Self Profile

In the Factor column, you will now have pages of pieces of your Self. They probably are not in much of an order, and you have only a vague sense of what all of these Self Factors might add up to. Your task now is to bring order out of this chaos and, not quite incidentally, create a profile of your Self. This Profile will help you remember what you are discovering about your Self and give you direction and support when some new issue hits.

I admit that I am aware of few men who have organized their Self Factors into a written Self Profile as mechanically as I have. Most men just let the pieces sit in their heads with whatever organization their brains provides. I found several advantages that came from the rather minimal effort it takes to pull a written Self Profile together at this point:

- It is much easier to remember, and therefore to express, your Self Factors when they're organized in to a Self Profile. This is particularly useful to have in the early stages of your journey from Required Masculinity to your Personal Masculinity.

- You will discover Self Factors that reinforce, expand, and enlarge each other.

- You will bring together Self Factors relating to a particular topic, and this can point you in useful directions for further explorations. When I saw music, theater, art, design, problem solving, and writing all together, I finally got the message: creativity is an essential Factor for me. From then on, I have pursued creativity wherever I could, to my constant pleasure and satisfaction.

Lay out all of your Investigation Sheets overlapped so that you see just the Factor columns. The Profile task will be easiest if you have access to a blackboard or whiteboard. Even a pad of large paper of the workshop variety will help. If nothing larger is at hand, put several pieces of regular paper out on the table in front of you.

You're going to transfer all of your Factors to the new pages, the pad, or the blackboard, grouping like Self Factors together. There are no correct or incorrect topics for these groups. Choose categories that reflect what you're discovering about your Self, and avoid categories that you think are "right" or "appropriate" or that you "should" have. It is crucial for you to do the grouping yourself, since each of your Self Factors carries hidden messages and meanings that only you can read. These messages are important elements in grouping your Factors. When you think you've got similar Factors, look again carefully. Different words or even a different order of the same words can reveal significantly different pieces of your Self.

When you've finished transferring all of your Factors into groups, you will have many groups of Self Factors. To refine your Profile even further, give each group a descriptive title as short as possible. Then, go back and review each title against the Factors listed in the group. See if you can make each group as narrow, consistent, and concrete as possible. At this point you might decide to combine some groups or split some groups. That's fine. You're after clarity and understanding about your Self here, not a prize for the neatest project. At the end, you will have your Self Profile.

It's your Self profile *pro tem*, for the moment. As useful as this first Profile will be, it isn't complete. The more of your Self you find the more you can add to your Profile. Any new experience, surprising feeling, challenge, or new perspective can trigger learning, new additions, and changes in your Profile. I completed my first Profile over ten years ago, and I still review it once every year or so to keep up with my changes, discoveries, and my current Self. I keep my typed Profile by my reading chair and use it as a place to begin when a new question hits or as a prod when I'm facing a new experience or test. Being able to get to my Profile at that moment keeps me on track and acting consistently with who I have discovered I am. The Profile also gives me a sword to use against Required Masculinity when it barges in, and it still does every so often.

Self-Profile building, like everything else, has its refinements. Very briefly, here are some of them:

- The more Events and Issues you add to your Investigation Sheets, the more pieces of your Self Factors you acquire, and the more accurate and useful your Self Profile will become.

- Repeated Factors indicate the strength of this Factor in your Self, or hint at some underlying Factor. Pay attention to these and follow their hints.

- What does *not* show up in your Self Profile can be a valuable piece of your Self – what you are not. Money and its issues had always driven at me, so I assumed that money would show up as a really important part of my Self. However, none of my Self Factors touched on money in any close way. It took me a long time to read this absence: my Self has no particular interest in money or its stakes (other than being able to live reasonably comfortably). My money concerns turned out to be just reflections of Required Masculinity and my mother's expectations. Of course, your missing piece could also be just the result of your never coming into serious contact with the issue.

- No Self Profile will have something to say about every conceivable topic or event in life. These blanks are okay, unless they occur where you have had actual life experiences. Then, such a blank suggests to me that you have probably been deeply hurt or frightened by this experience. Don't let these blank spaces sit there; tackle them, with a competent therapist if necessary. Often, important Self Factors are buried in these Events.

- You may find in your Profile single Factors, or even a whole group of them, which sound very much like Required Masculinity. Just because something is part of this masculinity doesn't mean it can't be part of your Self, but be very careful here. It's far more likely that this Factor is Required Masculinity sneaking in or a leftover Required Masculinity habit. If you end up with a Required Masculinity Factor, try cutting this Factor from your list. How badly do you feel without it? The worse you feel the more likely it is that this really is part of your Self. Another way to look at this kind of Factor is to compare the intentions with which Required Masculinity uses this Factor and the intentions with which you use it. These could cause you to restate the Factor more precisely.

- You may find in your Self Profile a piece that is, or when expressed is, violent, destructive, negative, or dangerous. Compare this one with the rest of your Self Profile. Is it inconsistent with everything else, or at least most of the other pieces, in your Profile? Will expressing this negative Factor prevent you from expressing other elements of your Self, or substantially interfere with you doing this? If you get a Yes to either of these questions, and particularly if you get two Yeses, this violence piece is probably not part of your Self but a trace of Required Masculinity training or some fear rooted very deeply in you. I encourage you to analyze this Factor thoroughly and then to define it more clearly. If you get any Noes, I would say that this violence Factor is a part of your Self, and you will need to figure out how to handle it. This could be just to keep an eye on it and to very carefully and consciously choose how you express it. Or, you could work with a therapist to reduce or eliminate its presence.

- If you find an "out in left field" Self Factor, you may be tempted to chuck your discovery into the trash as a mistake. It could, however, turn out to be your most exciting discovery about your Self. So, it is worth taking your time to understand this Factor and how it connects with the rest of what you learn about your Self.

Having completed your Self Investigation now, you know a lot about who you are.

You're also in a good position to effectively find and choose your own masculinity Tools and Intentions. This process is laid out in the next Challenge.

CHALLENGE #4:
FINDING MY MASCULINITY TOOLS AND INTENTIONS

Finding the Tools and Intentions that express your Self and you masculinity and putting them into use is what creates your Personal Masculinity. It's what makes you the man others see and rely on. It also sets up the dynamic for your relationships with our culture. This might be a good time to go back to The Words We Will Use Here (p. 5) and refresh your understanding of "Tools" and "Intentions". You find your Tools and Intentions by making your own search, arguments, and thinking, using what you now know about your Self. This will feel a bit like re-inventing the wheel and will require a lot of analyzing and creativity. An easier way is to look for various models of masculinity and to pick up the Tools and Intentions they have put together. What follows at this point is a collection of masculinities for you to consider as models for your Personal Masculinity. Once you pick your models, dig for the Tools and Intentions used by the models you choose. When you've found them, you have many pieces of your Personal Masculinity.

Masculinity Models

<u>The Virtuous Man.</u>

Okay, "virtuous" sounds sweet and a bit addled these days. I justify my choice of word because of a book I will mention in the next paragraph. In earlier centuries in Western culture, however, much was written and preached about the virtuous man, and many boys before the 1930s were raised with this model pushed at them. Why and how this form of masculinity died somewhere in the last century at the hands of corporate power, two world wars, and the rise of consumerism would make an interesting story, but in some other book.

What Is A Man? 3,000 Years of Wisdom On the Art of Manly Virtue (edited by Waller Newell) explores and describes the character of the virtuous man in a very large collection of excerpts, mostly from pre-twentieth century European, American, and Asian writings. Newell divides his selections by topic and introduces the selections for each topic with a brief essay on a particular type of virtuous man. To my summaries of Newell's essays I have added my comments in smaller type and centered. The last section of excerpts in Newell's book reflects the shattering of the traditional notions of the virtuous man by Required Masculinity. Since we've discussed Required Masculinity at length earlier in this book, I haven't summarized Newell's excerpts on this model.

Your response to these models may well be, "How quaint" and "How old fashioned," and to set them aside as hopelessly impractical and irrelevant. I encourage you not to turn your back on these and rush on, but to stop and give them your full attention for a while. Yes, they are ideal and, yes, in the years in which these virtuous models were consciously created, praised, and desired, their virtues were regularly and blatantly violated. On the other hand, I can think of few contemporary problems or situations in which men find themselves that wouldn't be improved significantly for that man and everyone else involved, if just a few of the men in the situation acted as virtuous men or at least tried to. Interestingly, young boys still seem to be innately in tune with many of these virtuous men. So, growing up in our present Required Masculinity culture is, in significant ways, about erasing this natural attraction to the virtuous man.

The chivalrous man. This is a man with refined manners, courtesy toward all, respect for women, and a character bred to the virtues of honor, courage, and self-restraint. Above all, it is about love of a woman who leads a man to moral decency.

> Beware of thinking of the chivalrous man only as a man clad in armor on a colorfully caparisoned horse fighting in a 14th century tournament in England or France. Consider him, instead, as a man who is respectful of each person he meets, who listens to each person and honors that person's needs and fears, and who plays fairly and honestly with everyone, a man for whom "fair" is a living force not just a whine. He is the man who seeks to preserve the rights and nurture the life of others, as well as of himself. He uses his skills and understandings courageously for ethical ends without having to win or get rich, and he gives ideals practical effect.

The gentleman. This is a man who knows how best to act in all circumstances, who is well-read with broad interests, who speaks thoughtfully and respectfully, and who presents himself modestly and respectfully to others.

> "Best" – now, there's a tricky word for us men today. It's slid from some impartial ideal, with all interests weighed, to something akin to "It benefits or agrees with me." "Best" is probably not "winning" to the Gentleman. It is not having control. It is rarely money. Hardest of all, of course, it is rarely something fixed and calculable. Instead, it expresses commitment

to ideals, a breadth of mind, an intention to improve. "Respect" sees you as one among many equals, not you at the top or you against many. It is expressing yourself neither more nor less than the people around you can express themselves. It is working fairly and directly with all of the competing needs and desires around you.

The wise man. This is a man who chooses to learn from all the experience life brings to him, who is willing to look beyond what he knows now to what he might know tomorrow, and who acts with deliberation and an intention to do the best he can.

The world of a wise man is a place of possibilities and perhaps. Certainty may be just for the moment, and he's ready to change it when a different view presents a fairer or clearer understanding. Reality, not rules, dogma, or expectations, forms his world and directs his actions, and reality is all of life's experience. I also see another important element hidden in this virtue: personal responsibility. He acts when his wisdom bids him act, not when other people command or expect him to act or when his own greed drives him to act. He accepts the consequences of his actions and softens the harm they may cause others.

The family man. This is a man with compassion, understanding, inspiration and patience; a man who actively cares deeply about the welfare of the people around him; and a man who devotes his time and energy to leading each of these people to be and do their best.

I particularly appreciate in this one the aptness of a Chinese proverb Newell includes in his essay on this man: "the family man should 'govern his family as you would cook a small fish – very carefully'." This lesson seems appropriate for every part of our lives. "Best", when applied to individuals, takes two forms: best expression of the individual, and best connection with others. Achieving both simultaneously is not easy and is sometimes impossible. Such is the price of being both an individual and a social being. Some men achieve both of these by seeking to balance them over a period of time and by always keeping this intention of balance in mind as they make their choices.

The kingly man. This is a man who defends and cultivates his community by serving the common good more than his own. A man who, with diligence, justice, and intelligence, works towards a well-ordered and fruitful society for all of its members, and who encourages and protects the learning, creativity, and the culture of his community.

Although Newell's book does not speak specifically of leadership, it seems to describe men who become leaders, none more so than the Kingly Man. This man deeply cares about who and what he affects. His relationship with people brings loyal followers and supporters and achieves much. Care for the community sounds a lot like altruism and suppressing yourself for the benefit of others. I see the virtue here as "contribute" where Required Masculinity says, "Manipulate to raise yourself". The Kingly Man, however, does not suppress his own character and skills and put others first; he refines his character and skills so that he can successfully bring others into shared community with him. This is a careful balance of his personal Self and the personal Selfs of others.

The noble man. This is a man who remains calmly true to his best nature under all circumstances, particularly when he creates harm unintentionally; who acts with dignity, compassion, generosity, honor, justice, and honesty; and who acts always to bring out the best in a situation and in the people affected by it.

Here's that word "best" again, but not just best for me (i.e., I win) but best for all of the persons affected (including me). This virtue moves the man's focus from him exclusively to him AND others. The Noble Man is perhaps best understood in the context of your natural Self. The Noble Man accepts calmly what his natural Self leads him to, even when this creates difficulties for him. For me, this is about my accepting responsibility for all of the consequences of my choices, whether I intended them or not. Blaming others, rationalizing consequences on the basis of The Great They or "forces beyond my control," or seeking revenge against someone is not The Nobel Man in action. This man works to repair the damage he causes and moves everyone forward as best he can.

The American man. This is a man who facilitates the freedom and dignity of every member of society, who encourages and supports each person in developing his or her capacities to their fullest extent, and who acts with self-reliance and makes his own choices.

Facilitating the freedom and dignity of every member of society requires respect, cooperation, and negotiation. Dominance Competition and control do not fit here. Neither does subservience, defeat, or harm. This man accepts that this balance is hard to achieve, but that it is worth working hard to gain. This is a man who does his own questioning and thinking, and questions himself first. He makes his own choices for everyone's interests based on reasons he finds valid. The "party line" pronouncements of The Great They, and even common sense, are all subjected to his own knowledge, standards, and intelligence. While he may disagree with the thinking and choices of others, or even dislike or fear them, he respects all choices honestly made.

Although a Virtuous man is rarely talked about these days, he is deeply embedded in our cultural history – the hero in the old Western movies, Western novels by authors like Zane Grey, and the fireman who risks his life to save the old lady in the burning building. He's the man who puts himself on the front line to protect the helpless and oppressed, to defend a community, and to right wrongs done by others. To him, power and control are not ways of getting control and money for himself, but ways to encourage everyone to find and lead their personal lives.

American Boy Scout Male.

When we reach high school, we men tend to toss Boy Scouts aside as part of the childhood we are definitely through with. I think, however, that we're much too eager to jump into Required Masculinity at that point to realize what we are tossing out.

The Boy Scout Oath:

"On my honor I will do my best
To do my duty to God and my country and to obey the Boy Scout Law;
To help other people at all times;
To keep myself physically strong, mentally awake, and morally straight."

Some will argue about the "God" part or about the "morally" part, but doing "his best" would certainly produce a very different community than the constant competition for power and money that Required Masculinity does. "Helping other people at all times" would lead a man to develop relationship skills that this masculinity demeans. Wouldn't "mentally awake" break the trance created by this masculinity and its exclusive focus on power and money?

The Boy Scout Law adds many more dimensions to the man who chooses to live by the Boy Scout Oath. This Law requires him to be:

Trustworthy	Loyal
Helpful	Courteous
Kind	Obedient
Cheerful	Thrifty
Brave	Clean
Reverent	

A man who fulfills these qualities would have the skills and motivation to be more cooperative, flexible, and probably more creative than the man caught in Required Masculinity. He'd probably be easier to live with, too, both for those around him and himself.

Finally, there is the motto we all love to make jokes about: "Be prepared". This is all about flexibility and adaptability, skills everyone needs in our current fast-changing world. If more men practiced this motto, they would probably be well on the road to finding more satisfying places for themselves in the present world. This motto is also about being alert to what is really going on around you. No "group think" here. No looking at the world in only one way. No using only the same-old methods for every situation.

The Men's Movement Male

Beginning in the mid-1980's, a men's movement grew up to raise awareness in men and women of the issues created by Required Masculinity. It reached its peak around the turn of the twenty-first century, but has been fading since. For twenty-five years plus, this movement stuttered over framing a notion of a masculinity that wasn't Required Masculinity.

This effort took several forms, reflecting various parts of the men's movement.

Archetype male. This is the mytho-poetic branch of the men's movement, most famously presented in *Iron John* by Robert Bly. It searches literature, psychology, and folklore for male archetypes. An archetype is a mental or psychological model expressing some generic, psychological, or spiritual fundamental male type. It is usually framed in terms of myths and beliefs, especially from the Greek and Roman cultures. The male archetypes are usually identified as the Warrior, the King, the Fool (the Trickster), and the Hero. In Michael Thomas Ford's *The Path of the Green Man*, he suggested another archetype, the Green Man, the man focused on his connection with his natural world. These intellectual constructs seek to identify and activate the most fundamental skills and perspectives in men. The mytho-poetic masculinity urges each man to study these archetypes and to choose one or a combination of them as a model for choosing his masculinity Tools and Intentions. The underlying belief here, as I understand it, is that, when a man aligns himself with an archetype, he draws into himself its natural and successfully tested strengths and abilities, which bring him a sense of internal strength and confidence.

A significant expression of this approach to manhood is the Men's Weekend. This event was, and perhaps still is, a Friday night through Sunday morning event in a resort or camp setting with fifty to one hundred men participating. Discussion groups on a variety of topics designed to draw out and explore each man's take on the topic fill much of the time. These topics range from What does Life want from me? to Can a real Man be an Artist? to How to Discipline My Kids Honestly. The evenings include dinners, one-on-one chats, talent shows, and relaxed games. Gossip by the media and others often makes fun of these weekends as "naked men running around in the woods beating drums". True, drumming and other Native American activities do often take place, and men sometimes do strip naked. They are stripping off the power and status of their daily Required Masculinity life in order to get down to their real selves. But, these are minor pieces of the weekend, if they occur at all. For most men attending these events, the trance of Required Masculinity is broken for the weekend, and they find permission to ask all the questions they've been carrying around for years about masculinity and who they really are.

Support group man. This approach to manhood is a process and attitude, not really a model of manhood. A men's support group has much the same purpose and process as a Men's Weekend, but it lasts just two hours on a weekly or monthly basis. Just as in the Weekend, a man can find and come to understand his issues as an individual male with the support and life experiences of other men. It is a place free of Required Masculinity judgment and compulsions and full of compassion, tolerance, and shared wisdom. For many a man, this may be the first time he has ever felt safe enough around other men to be absolutely honest about himself and to himself. It is probably also the first time he has associated with other men without the force of Required Masculinity being in control. He finds his own strength and his own answers by using the wisdom, experience, and encouragement of the men around him. He also experiences the deep satisfaction of being close to other men without giving or obeying orders and demands or competing for dominance. One of the benefits these men speak most often about is the experience of realizing that their tensions, worries, and fears are not just theirs, that all of the men in the room have or had the same tensions, worries, and fears. Being able to return weekly, or as needed, provides each man with steady encouragement and safety to build and practice new choices for his life, and receive male support and approval for them.

Men's rights man. This model of masculinity views males through the lens of the "inalienable rights" concept of the Declaration of Independence. It most often expresses itself primarily in political and legal actions. This shows up usually as a lawsuit that seems aggressively intent on restoring the unquestioned dominance of men and undoing the social, economic, and political gains made by women and others during the last forty years.

Father's rights man. This also doesn't provide a full model for masculinity, since it focuses on men only as fathers. It arises predominantly in the form of pro-father arguments raised against the strong bias of the courts and social services agencies in favor of mothers and against fathers in child-custody issues. These men assert that the father has as much importance and love for his children as the mother does and that custody issues and problems should treat mothers and fathers identically. In particular cases, it sometimes loses its impact and honesty, however, by arguing only the principle and ignoring a particular man's failure to adjust his Required Masculinity to act as a thoughtful and helpful parent with his children and to create an effective relationship with his ex-spouse. It is interesting, in an odd way, that the men who argue most strongly for their natural value as fathers seem to remain committed to Required Masculinity and make little effort to know or express their Personal Masculinities.

Living Male Model

As you look around you at the men in your world, you probably know a man or two who stands out because of his positive impact on everything around him, including you. The thought, "Boy, if I could be a man like he is", has probably flashed through your mind. Here is a good source from which you can model your own masculinity Tools and Intentions. To make this work, spend more time with him, get close to him if possible, and identify his priorities, how he treats people, and what he uses to make his choices. Ideally, you'll become friends, and you'll be able to ask some very specific questions or ask for direct advice on your own questions. Yes, this effort is a bit like studying an amoeba under a microscope, but there is no better way of learning what makes up his masculinity and what makes it work. This won't exempt you from digging for your own answers, but he will give you a tested, "feet on the ground," pattern as a starting point for finding and making your own choices. Once you've studied your man, you need to put your discoveries into precise and concrete words and concepts that speak in your terms. This will give you a concrete model to emulate. After this, it's a matter of being alert and putting all of this into regular practice in your own life.

The Hero

The Hero is the Male of all Males. He usually shows up in crisis situations, when a man needs to put everyone else always ahead of himself, which fortunately is not everyday life. However, he is only a man of the moment or, more precisely, the man of a specific situation, moment, and individual. No male is a Hero 24/7. If he tries that, he ends up a bully or such a monumental egotist that he is universally despised and ignored.

What makes a hero? Here are some elements to consider for your definition of "hero":

- The man knows his abilities (Tools) well, and is confident and effective in his use of them.

115

- He is willing and able to shift his Intentions fast from his usual choices to working for the benefit of others in need.

- He has the skills, stamina, and physical strength (Tools) to restrain the danger or rescue the victims from a large part of it.

- He focuses his Tools and Intentions on the facts and needs of the situation in which the danger is operating.

- He disciplines his actions and Tools to work efficiently towards achieving his protecting and saving Intentions.

An interesting question here might be: Which male is more apt, or more able, to step up to the challenge of a hero moment, a Required Masculinity male or a Personal Masculinity male? My guess is that a male that depends on the opinions of those around him (Required Masculinity male) is more apt to be controlled by their fears or mob action than by an independent assessment of the risks and needs around him. Living for sex, money, domination, and power doesn't seem very useful training for handling panic danger either. The Personal Masculinity male, on the other hand, is more apt to evaluate the crisis based on its reality and how the most threatened people can be helped.. Whether a particular man of this kind has the needed skills, strength, and stamina for a particular danger, however, is not a certainty.

Feminist Male Model

Masculinity has had no clear place in the issues of Feminism other than being the target of almost every complaint that the feminists throw out. The one thing their complaints do make clear is that women do not want Required Masculine types around. They are silent, however, about what they do want in their men.

bell hooks, a prolific feminist writer about the relationships of men and women, in *The Will To Change* complains at length about this silence. I examined *MS. Magazine* issues from 2000 – 2015 (winter) searching for feminism's desired qualities of masculinity. All I found in these issues was one feminist's experience of raising her son and a 1999 interview with two female authors of books studying the male condition. None of these authors provided anything remotely like a model of masculinity. In *Father Courage,* Suzanne Brown Levine looked at men and women very honestly, acknowledging that neither is totally saint or devil and that both have legitimate difficulties in making home and family a real partnership. This gave me hope of her identifying a Feminist-approved male model, but all she talked about was fathering. In *The End of Men and The Rise of Women*, Hanna Rosin shares a strong and surprising opinion from a number of the women she interviewed. These women won't consider any kind of relationship with a man who is employed less than fulltime in some dependable work. They also require him to take on some of the domestic and childcare tasks on his own volition. Some even insist that his income be close to hers, if not more. Neither of these authors said anything about any other Tools or Intention they, or women in general, want in a man.

Maybe we can find some of these by turning their complaints about men inside-out:

- "Men are enemies to be destroyed." Almost all of the men women experience are Required Masculinity males. So, presumably Feminism wants men to reject this masculinity totally, along with all of its Tools and Intentions, i.e., it wants the opposite of Required Masculinity.

- "Men don't do their share around the house." So, men better start learning a totally new set of skills. Housekeeping, kitchen skills, and child care skills are all learnable, of course, just as you learned how to operate a cell phone, fly a jet plane, or research and write a news report.

- "Men have no feelings." How much male feeling do they want us to display? My experience on this one tells me that the last thing women want is an emotional man on their hands. What they do want here eludes me completely.

- "He never says anything. He never talks about what's going on in his head or heart." This one is pretty vague. It could be just another version of He Has No Feelings, or it could be a demand reflecting the honest needs of relationship. Building a relationship requires a lot of sharing and mutual understanding. This can't happen when one or both of the people are tight-lipped, silent types. You've been trained for twenty-plus years by Required Masculinity to hide everything personal, admit no weakness or doubt, and silently soldier on. So, satisfying this piece of a Feminist masculinity will take a big change in behavior and attitude by you.

None of these reversals, as far as I can tell, is verbalized in Feminist literature, so they may well not be what the Feminists really want in a man. In *The Good Father,* Mark O'Connell discusses this absence of masculinity concept at length (pp. 22-37) and adds "sensitive man" and "Real man" to our Feminist fog.

Perhaps, this vagueness in Feminism's masculinity reflects an ambiguity in many women about the consequences of any kind of new masculinity. Maybe many women don't really want to initiate dates or sexual play or give up the protection men provide. Maybe they don't really want men to show their fears, and needs, and vulnerabilities. Maybe they don't really want to kill the mice, clean the eaves, or track down the noise in the night themselves. On the other hand, this ambiguity may reflect a much deeper problem. Women have been major trainers and enforcers of Required Masculinity, as well as major participants in the cultural force and propaganda machines that sells this masculinity. Maybe, like you, women have been so tied to this masculinity that they can't see any other model of masculinity either.

All we can do is hope that an individual woman is more specific about what she wants from your masculinity.

How To Do It

Making any kind of choice is a confusing task, and predicting what will work well in the future is impossible. But, standing there and dithering doesn't get you to your specific Tools and your specific Intentions. Do I start here or there, with this Tool or that one? Is this Intention more important to me than that one? Nothing will become clear until you dig your heels into something concrete.

Here's a possible concrete game plan for you:

First. Do your Self Investigation Sheets (Challenge #4). Another source of valuable information about yourself are the answers you wrote down to the questions in Appendix One and the scribbles, exclamation points, and underlinings you threw on these pages as you went along.

Second. Review your Self Factors and figure out the Tools you need in order to express your Self Factors and the Intentions with which you want to use these tools. This transformation could, of course, go on forever. So, to make this practical at the start, pick three important Factors, then identify the three Tools you most need to express each Factor and the primary Intention with which you want to carry out each Factor.

Third. Consider whether you want to use a masculinity model while you get your Tools and Intentions in working order.

Here's the list of models we went through earlier:

- The virtuous man,

    o The Chivalrous Man
    o The Gentleman
    o The Wise Man
    o The Family Man
    o The Kingly Man
    o The Noble Man
    o The American Man

- American Boy Scout Model
- Men's movement Models.
- Living Male Model.
- Feminist Male Model

Fourth. Are you going to stick totally with the model you picked, or do you not much like this model now? Remember there are still two other roads for you. One is to build your masculinity from scratch from what you're learning from your Self Investigation and your chosen Tools and Intentions. The other is to pick a bit from this model, a bit from that model, and some bits you invent from your Self and your chosen Tools and Intentions, and then blend this collection into a practical whole that you can express.

Fifth. Compare the masculinity you reached in Step Four and Required Masculinity. The worse the match-up, the stronger the message is that you should leave the world of Required Masculinity and follow your own choice. Challenge #2 discusses issues involved in making this break. It's only fair to warn you that leaving this masculinity will almost certainly raise mutterings, confusions, surprises, perhaps even some anger from people close to you. The best response to these is to explain your changes to them. At the very least, this will bring them up to speed on what you now understand about your Self and the questions you've worked through. Yes, there will still be adjustments to make and consequences to face, though they are probably much less threatening than you're imagining right now.

Getting this whole process moving can be hard since we're all a bit timid about making decisions, especially big ones like the ones this process pushes at you. Every decision, no matter how large or how unimportant, begins with one choice, just as every journey begins with one step. From my experience, it almost doesn't make any difference what your first step is. Once you've taken it, you will have one firm rock to stand on while you figure out your next step. One of the incidental, but very large, benefits from making this first choice is that you just took a whole bunch of options off the table, and you now have fewer things to think about. When you take the left-hand road at the fork, you can forget about whatever problems the right-hand road might have thrown at you. The more choices you make and the more your test them, the easier it all becomes and the more confident and faster you can make your choices and decisions.

The process at bottom is simple: Yes or No on each idea. On the other hand, I know from my own experiences doing this is a five-star difficult task, especially at the start. Difficult not only in the brain work but also in the emotional, practical, relational, and mental adjustments. I also know that you will doubt your sanity more than once during this process. However, other men have done this and I have done this, so I'm sure that you can, too. At the end, you will be more comfortable and satisfied with yourself and be a more effective male for those around you. Will you be done in a year? No. Three years? Probably not. Five years? Perhaps, although the experts say it takes ten years of concentrated effort to become a master of something. It took me all of ten years, but I had to discover most of the information and processes I lay out in this book as well as find my Personal Masculinity. My guess is you'll have your new man up and running in five years and running automatically and confidently in a couple of more years after that. Don't let this "five years" stop you. This isn't a 24/7 task, and gradually the work will disappear in the pleasure you'll get from your discoveries and the fading tensions and confusions along the way.

With all of these choices and questions in front of you, you're probably reeling, and this is beginning to feel like a nightmare. And, no doubt, Required Masculinity is looking more and more comfortable. I absolutely understand these feelings; I've been here. One day, you will stumble into a big surprise. That crushing demand to "be a Man" will have vanished, and who you are has become the only way you think. If this feels like jumping out of a plane now, don't look down, just focus on pulling the ripcord on your parachute. Focus on being the man you really want to be.

Then, follow that thread. I assure you that, if you stick with the effort, this thread will gradually grow into a sturdy Personal Masculinity that will carry you confidently into your life.

What If I Don't Like Where I End Up?

You are never locked in to anything – this is all your choice, beginning to end. If Choice #24 suddenly looks more important than Choice #1, this changes the game for you. Go back and re-run your process using what you learned in #24. If you find your choices work best using several pieces of several masculinity models, then use several and hammer together a masculinity that gives life to all of your choices. If your decision begins to stink, toss it out and start over. Maybe a decision works for two years and then doesn't. Nothing prevents you from rebuilding your choices and decision at that point. In all probability, at more than one time in your future, circumstances will force you to temporarily restrict the masculinity you have chosen, or even close it down, e.g., you want to work with horses but you suddenly discover you have an allergy to them or something in their environment, or you want to build furniture but you can't afford space for a shop or know how to run a necessary piece of equipment. When these circumstances pass, you can go back to the masculinity you decided on and see if it still works for you.

What Do I Do With My Personal Masculinity Choice?

Knowing your choice is not enough. Just thinking about your masculinity gets you nothing. Express it. Use it. Do it. Regardless of whether you choose Required Masculinity, one of the ready-made manhood models, or a unique package you devise for yourself, live your choice in as many thoughts and actions in every minute of every day as you can. Use your chosen Tools and Intentions constantly. Express them to others. Stand up for their validity and for yourself. Otherwise, your choices are only an intellectual game in your head and heart. Use them in exactly the same ways you have used Required Masculinity all these years. Use them to find your judgments, purposes, and directions. Use them to build relationships with your family, your community, your work mates, the country, and the world. Your masculinity choices can, and should, do all this for you.

If you can't express some Personal Masculinity choices on the fly, try building a specific action plan to follow. Take a piece of lined paper. Down the left-hand side of the page, list the Tools and Intentions of your chosen masculinity you want to express. Five or six of the ones you're most reluctant to express are enough for a start. Spread them out down the page so there are five or six lines between each of them. For each item on the left side, identify on the right side three to five specific ways in which you can express this one in your life. These ways can be anything, e.g., what you will say or won't say, what you will do or won't do, new organizations to join, job performance changes, new attitudes, not going somewhere any more, a new haircut, silly presents for yourself or a friend. The only requirement is that the action or statement expresses one of your chosen Tools or Intentions in a way that is clear to you.

This will give you a ready-made list of specific actions to take, instead of fumbling on the fly for how to change your behavior or, worse, forgetting to make the new choice altogether. This plan becomes a list of mental flags to get you moving on time – Oh, this is the staff meeting; I said I would protect the new employee. You have a detailed reminder of what you're trying to accomplish: I'm supposed to buy sexier clothes, not another sweat shirt. This also gives you a check list to use every once in a while to evaluate how your expression efforts are going. Do you give yourself an A or a C-, or an E for effort? Are you forgetting some of your Tools and Intentions more often than not, usually the unfamiliar ones?

If you are unsure about your determination and dependability on this live-my-masculinity project, go through the items in your action plan and put specific dates and places, and even times if necessary, on each one and use the list as a schedule. Keep the plan with you in your briefcase or pocket, beside your favorite chair, in the car – or, better yet, in all three places. Look at it a couple of times a day as a tool to bolster your nerves, keep your change moving forward, and to give you cause to cheer your progress. There will be progress, and it will increase with every expression of your masculinity you make.

Making the move from Required Masculinity to your Personal Masculinity is just like learning anything. At first, everything is an effort; it feels like you're trying to move a mountain. Then, one day you move that mountain a bit here and a bit there. Then, you've got the whole mountain moving. Finally, the mountain seems to disappear, and you're in the place where you want to be.

The hardest part of this live-my-masculinity process is expressing your choice the first couple of times. Probably, your first step away from Required Masculinity and expressing your own masculinity will be so small or accidental that you will be unaware of it. I'm sure that my first step was. I suspect it was some quiet, internal No to something Required Masculinity demanded. My internal system then said, Aha, I got away with that one, so let's try this one. Somewhere in one of the early, little steps of mine,

I discovered that Required Masculinity is so muscle bound and obsessed with its own power and glory that it easily misses my small escapes. Where once I was sure that there was nothing outside of Required Masculinity, I gradually found solid ground and breathtaking opportunities.

The excitement of this change can carry you away, so exercise a little careful thought about your early expressions of it. In the early months, you don't have a very complete understanding of your Self or your chosen masculinity choices, and meeting intense opposition can badly rattle your fragile early confidence in them and in the process you're relying on. I, however, did not follow this good advice. When I accepted that color, particularly bright color, was part of my Self, this discovery so excited me that I wanted to express it ASAP. I chose to first express it in a bank, in the "front line", at a teller station (one of my part time jobs at that time). I'm glad to report that my bright red shirt one morning did not get me fired or demoted. Or, even sent home for a "proper" shirt (much to my surprise). Instead, I collected cheers from the other tellers and the customers and a tolerant smile from my branch manager. The fact that this was a bank in a small city in Vermont no doubt helped my breakout enormously. I doubt that my red shirt would have been so well-received on State Street in Boston or LaSalle Street in Chicago. It felt wonderful expressing color, me, to my world that day. Even better was discovering that I could get away with it.

Breaking out of Required Masculinity and moving into your own masculinity choices requires you to shift your old perspectives and to make a lot of changes. This may also seem to require more strength and independence than you have. Not to fear. From the stories told by men in my groups, your desires for your new way of living will give you more than you need of everything to make this break and to settle yourself in your own masculinity. One of the harder changes you will have to cope with will be the loss of the shield against personal responsibility that Required Masculinity has provided for years. Behind this shield, we could look at a consequence and say, "Hey, I'm a Man. I did what I was expected to do," and shrug off personal responsibility for it. When we're outside of Required Masculinity and in our Personal Masculinities, there is no "expected" to cover us, and we must take responsibility for the consequences ourselves. This loss of protection forces me to think seriously about potential consequences as I make choices to express my Self. This was a bit terrifying at first, but I have discovered that my Personal Masculinity was much, much less dangerous to others than Required Masculinity. So, I had many fewer negative consequences to worry about than I expected. I also discovered that doing something out of the Required Masculinity mold so stunned some people that they couldn't respond at all to my choice. By the time they could, they realized that my new behavior was no threat to them or the world.

Learning to express your masculinity choices will be like following a diet or exercise plan: the more you do it, the easier it becomes for you and everyone around you and the fewer fears you will experience. One day, as you sit down to dinner, you will suddenly realize that you expressed your choices that day without thinking about them. Sometime later, it will hit you that you're living your choices more often than Required Masculinity's expectations. Finally, you will live your choices as totally and with as little thought as you breathe, just as you used to live Required Masculinity. Then, of course, you'll have only yourself to tackle when you're not happy with your life.

CHALLENGE #5:
MY EMOTIONS

Men And Emotion

Required Masculinity says, "No emotions. They're weak and girlish. They're valueless distractions from the goals and actions of a real Man. If you have them, suppress and ignore them." End of subject.

Daily experience, mine and yours, on the other hand, tells us clearly that we have emotions. We laugh, and panic, and yearn, and get shocked, and snicker many times a day, but maybe only inside. In the last five days, have you found yourself experiencing any of these?

Tensed up	Relaxed
Smiling	Frowning
Holding your breath	Enjoying something
Remembering something you liked	Avoiding something
Touching someone with meaning	Laughing
Wanting to cry or scream	Pounding the table or wall
Wanting to leap for joy	Growling at someone

Each of these reactions expresses an emotion you experienced in that moment. Undoubtedly, you expressed your emotions in many other ways as well. Emotions are regular and often large pieces of you and me as human beings. Required Masculinity, however, demands that we deny all this. Daniel Goleman, in his book *Emotional Intelligence*, says, "A view of human nature that ignores the power of emotions is sadly short-sighted". Each emotion has something to tell you, affects you immediately, and probably produces consequences you have to manage in one way or another for days, if not years.

All of us men remember our emotions when we were boys. Those emotions didn't go away; we just got really good at suppressing them or ignoring them in order to be part of Required Masculinity. Almost every man I know at all well has hidden one or two deep emotional loads all of his life. Even if you don't think you have an emotion in your body, your brain configuration does have an emotion component. Since it exists, you have emotions and can't eliminate them. With constant practice, however, you've trained another part of your brain to slam and lock the door on the emotion part. So, like a car buried in a snowdrift, you can dig out your emotion part any time you want to and get it running.

Most men not only think that emotions are bad, they think that emotions are just the negative ones, e.g., hate, fear, dislike, sadness. Positive emotions, e.g., joy, contentment, humor, love, usually get no thought from us at all. Required Masculinity allows us anger, but never labels this as an emotion. Instead, it says, "Anger is Manly power." Emotions, however, are not just negative. Goleman points out that each emotion comes in a continuum of strengths.

Anger	from irritation to fury
Sadness	from cheerlessness to deep depression
Fear	from worry to panic
Enjoyment	from pleasure to ecstasy
Love	from acceptance to infatuation
Surprise	from awe to shock
Disgust	from dislike to revulsion
Shame	from chagrin to guilt

(*Emotional Intelligence*, 28)

We complicate our emotion issue by having different words for various points along one of these continuums. Think of anger ... pique, dislike, resentment, upset, ire, rage, fury. This tends to confuse us into thinking that there are just too many emotions for us, especially men, to understand and deal with.

Another thing many of us, especially we men again, forget about emotion is that it's a communications system to us. This can be simple and straightforward: you fear the lion because it might kill you, and this tells you that your life is very important and had better be protected. Or it can be deep and complex: you enjoy watching pornography and this message might be telling you that sexual intimacy is important enough to you that you do it even though your over-bearing father condemns it. Your infatuation with a picture may have little to do with the picture, but is telling you that your life badly needs a change: get out of the city and live along the ocean, dump the white walls in your house and get some color into your life, track down the old friend who looks like the man in the picture and rebuild a friendship you once cherished. Maybe you can catch the emotion's message yourself, or maybe you need the help of a therapist. Either way, your efforts to find the message in your emotion will be worth your effort to find it.

What Men Know About Their Emotions

Very little. Required Masculinity and all of its teachers, trainers, and enforcers never taught us about emotions or even let us learn on our own. "They're girly, weak." This shut down began with that shout none of us ever forgets, "Boys don't cry. Don't be a sissy." As a result, many of us often can't even name an emotion when we have one. We don't know the words or what feelings they label, or what triggers them, or how they play out in us, or anything else. This non-education, of course, doesn't prevent us from experiencing lots of emotions.

In the absence of emotional knowledge, we still have to come up with some way of dealing with the emotions we can't escape. The male default method, according to many experts, is to use anger. Or maybe, since Required Masculinity sort of approves of anger, it is just the only thing available to men. So regularly do men express anger that many researchers suspect that we men turn all of our emotions into anger and use angry outbursts as a way of releasing at least some of the energy created by whatever emotion we feel. As any man can testify, of course, anger rarely really settles the emotion we have. And, more often than not, it hides the emotion even more from us, leaving it to roll around inside us and disrupt nearly everything. Even worse, anger misdirects us. Anger means blame and fault, but these are almost always irrelevant to what our emotion is really about. These just focus us on external causes rather than our internal conditions which are the sources of our emotions. In desperation, many of us just slam the door on the whole thing.

As a result of this emotional ignorance, men struggle with "How do I cope with what's going on inside me?" most of their lives. How do I manage the impact of this on my driving, my work, my co-workers, my family, the stranger who triggered this feeling? What do I do now? Lost in this struggle, a man is at risk to be easily manipulated or of having valuable information hidden from him. Worst of all, he sets himself up for that awful question, "What kind of Man am I?" and a big negative answer.

Learning About Your Emotions

If you were still only 1 or 2 years old, you could learn about them as easily as your sister does or mother did. They were cuddled and cooed over and allowed, even expected, to show all their feelings. Your sister was encouraged to talk about her feelings and given the words to do it, to analyze her feelings and read the feelings of others, and to let emotions inform her choices and actions. In the process, she built her emotional literacy. If you are still ten or twelve, maybe you could still learn this way, too.

At twenty-five, or forty, or fifty, however, you'll have to teach yourself in an intellectual way. Goleman's *Emotional Intelligence* would be a good first textbook. Another option is to search in your region, particularly if it is urban or has colleges and universities, for workshops and retreats to develop emotional intelligence. Psychotherapists and counselors can also help on a one-to-one basis.

The core of what you need to learn, however you learn it, is the following:

- The vocabulary to name your various feelings.

- The way each emotion shows up in your internal sensations.

- What sets off each emotion and what this trigger tells you about your Self and the situation in which you find yourself when the feeling hits.

- How to manage the power of each emotion in order to control the harm and to use it productively.

- How to use your emotions to motivate yourself.

- How to recognize emotions in others and interpret them.

- How to integrate your emotions and the emotions of others to build relationships.
  (See also, *Emotional Intelligence,* p. 43 and following.)

In reality, of course, no one succeeds on all of these points with every emotion in every instance. However, the more of these you master, the less frightening, more manageable, and more useful your feelings will become for you. You can become as comfortable with your emotions as you are with your intelligence, physical abilities, or any other part of your Self. Gaining emotional literacy, however, takes the same kind of effort and intention as gaining any other skill, e.g., willingness, perseverance, learning, tolerance for stepping off the cliff to try your new wings, practice (lots of it), and determination. Most of all, no literacy happens if it remains just an intellectual theory; you need to be use it, a lot.

The further you step away from Required Masculinity into your Personal Masculinity, the easier time you probably will have in building your emotional intelligence and in figuring out how to live it. So, I encourage you to disconnect from a lot of Required Masculinity before you tackle building your emotional intelligence.

CHALLENGE # 6:
COPING WITH CONFLICT

Violence and male is one of the quickest links most people make in our culture. Male violence seems to be driven by Required Masculinity's obsession with control, power, and Dominance Competition. It easily pushes a disagreement into a fight over control, power, and Dominance Competition by throwing "Who's going to be a real Man here" in one man's face. This manipulation drives stress into road rage. Games into bloodthirsty attacks on the field and in the stands. Legislative debate into personal power plays. Disagreements into street knife fights and barroom brawls. The actual issues in these conflicts, of course, get totally lost by this twist into masculinity testing. The rest of us have to deal with the men's irrelevant games as well as the still unresolved issues. And, the men end up with severely limited understandings of their own manhoods.

Say "male violence", and the first thought of most people is male violence against women. The level of male violence against men, however, is several times the level of men's violence against women, and it takes the form of shooting and homicide in an appalling number of cases. Males are 3.5 times more likely than females to be murdered in the United States (2012). Homicide is the second leading cause of death for men 15-24, and third leading cause for men 25-34 (2010). It's generally reported that 5%-14% of American men, during their lifetimes, will be sexually assaulted, and the number is much higher in prison populations. Most of these assaults on men are by heterosexual men. Among young, impoverished, and under-educated men, the violence figures are staggering. The silence of our culture in the face of this, however, seems to say, "Go ahead, do what you want to men. Men are of no more value to us than the newspaper we wrap the garbage in."

Violence is so associated in our minds with beating up people or shooting them that merely abusive behaviors, e.g., sexual abuse and psychological abuse, usually escape condemnation or often even identification. Some could easily argue that the sneering, "Are you a Man or a sissy", thrown at a male, is psychological abuse. The impact of this "unseen" violence can be greater in many ways than physical violence and is often harder to heal. Some men who pride themselves on avoiding physical violence, however, toss out "I never touched her" and feel totally free to express their Required Masculinity using these "unseen" methods.

Reasons For Violence

Brain theory. Many brain theory scientists claim that the male brain is particularly configured for spatial and physical action, which makes men more prone to and more capable of physical violence. (See also page 24.)

Copulation opportunities. Some people argue that male violence is tied to the limited number of females available for copulation. Some men have certainly used violence to gain copulation opportunities and to control their women, though it's doubtful to me that just the numbers of women are the cause. Although the United States Census Bureau statistics (2010) show that males in the United States outnumber females until their early 30s, the two genders are approximately equal in numbers for the next ten years. Females increasingly out-number males for their remaining years. Even during their high copulation years, most men know, or at least quickly learn, that violence never gets them the kind of sex they want, nor do most of us men use violence for this purpose.

Cultural tolerance. Most people tend to accept men's violent behavior as a reasonable way for them to express anger and male emotion generally. This enables men to largely escape accountability for either the degree of their violence, its kind, or the motives hidden behind their violence. In some settings, e.g., football and hockey, violence is even specifically praised and enjoyed.

Defend honor. The world has a long history of men using violence to "defend their honor", i.e., to protect their power.

Genetics. People often argue that male violence is simply male genetics in action. Michael Kimmel, a social scientist who writes often on men's issues, takes a contrary position: "The belief that violence is manly is not carried in any chromosome, not soldered into the wiring of right or left hemispheres, not juiced by testosterone. … Boys learned it … from their fathers … from a media that glorifies it, from sports heroes who commit felonies and get big contracts, from a culture saturated in images of heroes and redemptive violence." (Quoted in Klein, *The Bully Society* p. 55.)

Humans are animals. In his book, *The Professor in the Cage: Why Men Fight and Why We Like to Watch* (2015), Jonathan Gottschall argues that human beings at their core are animals, male animals are violent, and so we should expect male humans to be violent. He sees this as inescapable biology. Human beings, of course, are biologically like animals in many ways, but they have substantial thinking and communication capacities that animals do not. We are nearly unique in the animal world for the capacities of our brains, and we have learned to use this brain-power very adeptly and easily. To tell a male human that his brain cannot and should not control his physical actions, which Gottschall and others seem to say, denies you and me of at least half of the being we are.

It's a male thing. Gottschall, although an English Professor, took up Mixed Martial Arts for several years. This is a form of no-holds barred fighting between two men in a cage until one man signals he quits. As Gottschall describes these fights, they are brutal, often with serious physical damage. The extensive training for this is done in a gym setting among a group of men, and major fight events are done in a public space with many invited spectators. The fact that some men volunteer for this violence or cheer for it does not make it a requirement for manliness or even a common male pastime. If all males were this violent all the time, we humans would long since have destroyed ourselves. In any event, I doubt that many people would say that the behavior of a minority of males should set the definition for "male human".

Military training. The military is all about violence. Its intentions and efforts, however, are directed at keeping the violence headed at a dangerous enemy and contained to war zones and training grounds. However, the effects of military violence often spread far in to our families and communities.

Required Masculinity. Required Masculinity does not explicitly demand violence, Although physical violence is often the way the rewards promised by Required Masculinity are gained. Lest we overlook it, this masculinity does not ban violence or even discourage it, or give primacy to meeting the real needs of a situation.

The strongest argument against all of these rationalizations for male violence is the unavoidable fact that this violence is not a universal male trait. Most men are rarely violent in their entire lives. Even men who are regularly violent are not violent all the time. Even men eagerly committed to Required Masculinity do not push into extreme, violent masculinity all the time, or even most of the time. Is male violence, then, some aberration caused by a confluence of certain planets in the heavens? Some studies indicate that a man's decision to be violent is a reflection of his experience growing up. However, violence is rarely a universal rule even for a man with this background.

A man who lives in a network of people who accept violence or reward violence tends to be more prone to use violence, but even he won't be constantly violent.

Over the years that I've searched through this male violence fog, I've come to wonder if this violence is mostly a matter of a man's lack of knowing who he really is and how to express this. Is he like a sailboat without a rudder that the winds bang around and eventually crash into someone or something? When a man knows his choice of Tools and Intentions and can express these, will violence be of much interest to him?

For some men, violence is totally avoided because of the horrendous costs it usually brings, e.g., physical injury, loss of job, loss of love and family, exile from friends and community, revenge attacks, jail, death. Yes, we all have our moments of anger and frustration and feel a need to strike out physically. But, most of us rarely do or do so only when we're alone. This reluctance to step into violence is not lack of maleness, but a reflection of the host of other forces that rest within us. These include: our ability to control instincts and to act after weighing pros and cons; the values we place on family, friends, community, workmates, and other people in our networks; our goals, pleasures, and desires; the things or actions that inspire and excite us. You and I are not less male, in any reasonable sense of this word, when we choose to follow these forces instead of violence.

The Value Of Violence And Dominance Competition

Let's admit that violence and Dominance Competition have some very strong attractions for men of the Required Masculinity persuasion. First of all, these succeed magnificently on occasion in turning nobodies into somebodies, i.e., gives the winner power and often wealth. Second, these, unquestionably, are the most exciting expression of Required Masculinity there are. Third, these use many of the major masculinity Tools: physical motion, problem solving, hands-on action. Fourth, these are the ultimate form of anger, that emotion our culture seems to expect and want from men. And, finally, the Required Masculinity system really enjoys these.

In part, violence and Dominance Competition are common because arguments against them are rarely voiced persuasively or consistently. This seems very strange given the vast number of children, adults, businesses, and communities harmed by the results of these. It looks even stranger when you realize that most of the victims of these behaviors are men themselves. Occasionally, winners speak against violence and Dominance Competition, but these speeches normally come only long after the fact, when experience and wisdom have persuaded these winners that their glorious win came at too much cost. These speeches against violence and Dominance Competition also come too quietly to stop the juggernaut of Required Masculinity's constant preaching that these forces are the only Manly responses to challenge and disagreement.

Resolving Conflicts

Men, and our culture, do not always resort to violence and Dominance Competition to resolve conflicts. They have created a number of alternatives to these, though they often ignore or hide these methods and drag them out only as last resorts. In any event, these alternative methods of conflict settlement are certainly not approved by Required Masculinity, since they effectively undermine the control, Dominance Competition, and power it preaches.

Prevention. Prevention requires that you understand a potential conflict in as many ways as you can long before it actually appears. You, then, design a course of action that eliminates or substantially reduces the conflict or its causes, and act accordingly. Since few of us are totally omniscient, preventing every possible conflict in our lives, even in a specific situation, is probably unlikely. However, preventing even half of them is valuable.

Avoidance. Just swallow your ego and ignore Required Masculinity or decide the issue isn't important enough to fight about – and walk away. Often we accept hierarchy and the authority of position as an excuse to avoid a conflict: "Can't fight City Hall." Avoidance, of course, almost never really settles the conflict, though it evades the harms violence usually brings.

Negotiation. You recognize a conflict for what it is, and you and the other party talk through this conflict, its issues, and how the two of you can either settle them or move around them. This removes the conflict before there's an excuse for someone to throw that Are You A Man question on the table. This negotiation is best written down to record the terms by which a conflict has been or will be settled. Written down, the agreement can be accurately remembered and, if necessary, enforced. The written document can be in almost any form. It just needs to contain the terms and the signatures of each party expected to abide by those terms. In many ways, negotiation and contract is conflict avoidance, or at least conflict reduction in advance.

Purchase. You buy out the other person's interest in the conflict, either permanently or for a specific time or place. Wages and salary buy out your desire for free time and activities of your choice. My neighbor pays me for a right-of-way over my land so that he can get to the street without a fight. You pay the storeowner so that you can take the flat screen TV out of the store without a contest and the police. The United States promises military hardware to some country in exchange for letting the US military use some of that country's territory.

Mediation. Those in the conflict bring in a neutral third party to help them understand the issues in the conflict, identify and value possible solutions, and make choices that work for all the parties. As in negotiation, the parties to the conflict make the final decision. The third party brings an objective view to the issues and potential solutions, which broadens everyone's understanding of the conflict, widens the options put on the table, and cools the heat in the conflict. This method rarely works, however, if the Are You A Man question has already been thrown into the conflict. Also, mediation works well on facts, but poorly when emotions are in control of the situation.

Arbitration. Those in the conflict bring in a third party and turn over the conflict to that person. They agree to abide by whatever the arbitrator decides. The arbitrator investigates the conflict and delivers a solution the arbitrator thinks will work best to get everyone moving again. The parties to the conflict give up their ability to control the investigation, the options, and the final decision, except to the extent that they can persuade the arbitrator. This process totally undermines the Required Masculinity on both sides of the conflict. How wedded each side of the conflict is to Required Masculinity, however, has a huge impact on whether arbitration is even possible.

Lawsuit. In European history, the lawsuit was created to stop physical fighting, lethal Dominance Competition, and a range of conflict resolution methods we would brand today as mystical, mythical, or just plain bizarre.

It substitutes strict procedures, principles, and words for a physical fight for control. Almost fifteen hundred years later, the Anglo-American legal system has mixed success at resolving conflicts in the face of Required Masculinity. Its success largely comes from the contestants choosing to accept the court decision as the end of the conflict. In this way, a lawsuit is like arbitration. Unfortunately, current costs, complexities, and time delays of a lawsuit usually make it an option of late, if not last, and expensive resort.

Legislation. Taking an issue into the political process of a legislative body is the way that many large public conflicts have been resolved. It is rare, but not impossible, for private conflicts to be handled this way. Since legislation applies to the entire community (local, state, or national), the solutions legislated usually are arbitrary and universal in comparison to a particular conflict. In the specific situation, this often creates more conflict than solution. In recent years, unfortunately, this legislative process to resolve conflicts has been substantially destroyed by politics in the Required Masculinity style.

Regulation. There are two kinds of regulations for resolving conflicts. One is governmental regulation. For the most part, these regulations, like legislation, apply largely to public conflicts. They are created by a governmental bureaucrat in accordance with the dictates of legislation and have much the same effect as legislation. The other kind of regulation is the whole range of policies and procedures created in businesses, institutions, and other organizations to manage their affairs.

Most of these dispute alternatives aren't of much use, however, in office politics, parking place stealing, or neighbor arguments. In the end, you will probably face a rock and hard place. The rock: if the other guy is determined to play Required Masculinity, you can't stop him. The hard place: you have to choose how you're going to respond, with Required Masculinity or your Personal Masculinity. It is likely that your Personal Masculinity will let you find a way out of or around the conflict and to an answer to the real cause of the conflict. Required Masculinity will likely heighten the conflict and increase the probability of harm to both of you.

The only long term way to reduce male violence is the same one needed to reduce male violence in the domestic setting: our culture needs to shut down Required Masculinity and help men select other kinds of Tools and Intentions to use in conflict situations. Were this to happen, we could also deal more honestly and directly with the disagreements causing the conflicts. Unfortunately, I'm doubtful that our present culture will make this radical a change any time soon, which leaves you and me with the rock and the hard place to deal with.

CHALLENGE # 7:
ENDING MY LONELINESS

"I'm so lonely" was often one of the first things a new man in my support groups said about himself. It seemed to make no difference whether he was straight, gay, bi-; married, single, divorced, a widower; his age; working, self-employed, or unemployed; of white or some other ethnicity. Even when he could point to large families, circles of friends, and friendly co-workers in his life, he still felt lonely. From the way these men reacted to the relaxed safety he felt in the support group, my guess is that his loneliness was not about physical isolation, but the absence of close, deep, and safe emotional and psychological communication with one

arl Erikson

or two other men. When this subject came up, men often spoke enviously of the close female connections they see their wives, girlfriends, daughters, mothers, and sisters have and seem to keep so easily. Steven Botkin described the reality of this deep desire of man as: "In each gesture of domination or control can also be found the agonized and distorted reaching for contact that is struggling to break through the legacy of hidden pain and fear" (*Voice Male*, 50).

Many people deny the idea that men are lonely, pointing to amateur baseball and soccer leagues, "nights out with the boys", Kiwanis, fraternities, hunting trips, evening beers with office and factory mates, and shared spectator times at sporting events. Yes, men there are physically together with other men. However, let's look carefully at what actually happens in these male outings. Required Masculinity rules are in full play here, with their usual results. There is plenty of activity, noise, and talk, but the hanging sword of Required Masculinity stifles much heart-to-heart, trusting, open friendship between men. How many men leave these gatherings for home feeling really connected to another man in the group and totally safe with him? I don't deny that some men in some of these groups do find deep friendship, but the experiences of many men say that these groups are more façades or "prove you're a Man" sessions than substantial personal connections.

Look at that most basic connection between men in our culture, the handshake. It is at arm's length. It is brief. It involves our furthermost extremities, our fingers. Often it becomes a contest over who can grip the hardest. In most cases, it is entirely formal and devoid of thought and attention. Originally, its only purpose was to prove that neither of you was armed, but almost no man uses it this way today (even when he is armed). Ordinary American men are usually shocked to their core by the hugs and kisses exchanged with enthusiasm between Spanish, Greek, Italian, and Arabic men. Maybe an arm across the shoulder is okay, as long as it congratulates and doesn't stay long. The pat on a man's ass is acceptable, if it's mostly hidden in some athletic moment.

We men, however, are not natural loners, as any man's childhood will attest. The occasional friends who last from grade school, high school, or college also show that men can seriously connect with other males. Even as adults, men occasionally form close friendships. Pointing also to the fact that most men marry or at least date seriously, most people argue that male loneliness is nonsense. Where, then, do all these lonely feelings in men come from?

Sources Of Loneliness

Consider these:

- Required Masculinity's demand that a man never be dependent on anyone; "A real Man doesn't need anybody".

- Required Masculinity says that the way to relate to another man is to dominate him, have more money and power than he does, or prove you're physically stronger than he is – or, best of all, all three ways.

- Men's ignorance of emotions in general (his and hers) and of how to act in the presence of emotions (Challenge #5).

- Required Masculinity tells you and me that a Man should dominate a woman and that his relationship with her must be all about sex and control.

- The judgment of our culture and of Required Masculinity for eons has been that any real friendship with another man makes them both homosexual.

Does it take an astrophysicist to recognize that we cannot create deep friendship with these rules in place? When we get beaten, dominated, or ignored, do we smile and ask him to join us for a hike? No, we flee or throw up walls. Driven apart by all of these forces, where is a man to go but into emotional or even physical isolation?

Often the only person even close to a friend for a man is his female partner or spouse. This rarely ends his loneliness because all of the forces I just described are still operating at full strength. Men are very skilled at hiding these from women, but their impacts remain in escapable. To the extent a man gets a good intimate relationship with a woman, he is probably dependent on her to give, and I emphasize "give", him this relationship. Relying on a woman to satisfy this basic need often leads to one if two not results. Either, the man requires so much to meet his needs for connection that he exhausts the woman, who then walks away for her own survival. Or, the man, relying on the relationship = sex formula of Required Masculinity, turns the relationship into a predominantly sexual one, which does not meet the woman's other needs and desires and she walks away. With her death or departure, of course, the man usually loses even this small connection and ends up wandering alone until he finds a therapist to provide sympathy and encouragement to him.

Before we move on, homophobia needs some specific attention. Like smoke, homophobia curls silently through the world of men. It's denied by everyone, but it is incessantly present. The dictionary defines homophobia as an unreasoning fear of or antipathy toward homosexuals and homosexuality. In the male world, "homophobia" carries a much broader meaning than this. It's a judgment that the other man fails to act as Required Masculinity demands and the speaker condemns and derides this man. It is not a comment about the other man's sexual choice, but about the other man's acts, what he wears, what he likes, what he reads or listens to or watches, what his priorities are, and what he says. This homophobia shouts "gay", "homo", and "fag" often, with sexual additions blunt enough to be considered sexual harassment if they were aimed at a woman. In our offices, gyms, arenas, and on the street, however, the shouter is rarely seen as vicious, just mildly impolite; he's "just being a Man". Even two men speaking quietly together or walking together can trigger these shouts and condemnations. Or worse. In 2008 a man was shot for walking arm in arm with his brother, and an 8th grade boy was shot for giving a male classmate a Valentine card (*Voice Male*, 117). The energy and anger that delivers these homophobic accusations would in other contexts probably lead a bystander to wonder about the speaker's mental condition.

No small amount of hypocrisy is alive and well in this "street" homophobia. Among the strongest shouters in this homophobia game often are men in organizations tightly committed to Required Masculinity, e.g., gangs, the military, sports teams. However, from anecdotes we've all heard or read, we know that there are deep male friendships in these organizations and open expressions of these connections. What they condemn on the street, they indulge in the closet created by these organizations. I wouldn't be surprised if many "fag" shouters also had male friendships in their youth which they still treasure.

With the current growing public acknowledgement and acceptance of gays in this country, we can hope that the steady judgments of "homo", "fag", and "gay" will fade, and take this part of Required Masculinity with them. Until the enormous power of Required Masculinity in our culture is cut way down, though, I suspect that the current homophobic condemnations will not weaken however much the shouting of them does.

Elements Of A Good Relationship For A Man

We all use "good relationship" the same way we say, "Take care," when we part: we don't think much about what it means. Is the problem of "good relationship" that we men can't find one, or that we have no idea of what a "good relationship" is? I'd say that men not knowing what makes a good relationship multiplies the power of the anti-friendship rules of Required Masculinity. So, what make a "good relationship" for a man, for you?

You are not totally ignorant of what a good relationship is. Human beings are social creatures. By trial and error over the eons, we men have discovered much about this connection thing. We have watched how the few good relationships we know operate. In special moments, we've talked with others about what a good relationship is. Most of us, in our youth or teenage years, had a buddy or two with whom we did as much as we could, certainly all the things we thought were important to us. Years later, we often longingly look back at this satisfying and easily maintained relationship, wanting desperately to have another one just like it. Some men are lucky enough to have had a work relationship somewhere along the way which expanded into support during his child's operation or his friend's divorce. Maybe you even had a client or customer relationship that let you be both totally honest and more than a little bit silly with each other. All of these experiences point you to some of what a good relationship can be.

"Relationship", like "big", covers a whole range of connections, e.g., a joking exchange with your favorite bank clerk, a fake insult-throwing relationship with your next-door neighbor, an awestruck apprentice-mentor relationship, a passionate sexual connection, a "let's go to the movies (or game, or art show)" relationship, a relationship of mutual trust, openness, and understanding. And, for each of us, there is the deepest and most intimate relationship of all, love, with all of its joys and sorrows. Which of these or a host of other variations, is the "good relationship" you want? In all likelihood, you'll also need to ask this question for each person you want to have a relationship with. At the heart of these relationships seem to be a few core factors:

- Total respect and trust. Not without challenge or debate on occasion, but always this as the starting point and ending point.

- Total absence of Dominance Competition, but probably a lot of moderate Testing Competition.

- Safety, physical and in many other ways.

- Encouragement and support, e.g., a sharing of skills, time, wisdom, and knowledge.

How these show up in the details of a relationship, of course, depends entirely on who you are and who your friend is. These are way beyond my ability to guess; the two of you have to dig these out yourselves. Since many men look with envy at the relationships their wives and girlfriends have with their circle of women friends, maybe you could ask them to teach you some of the skills she and her friends use to make their relationships with each other work.

Finding Good Relationships

Start with the obvious. Since most of your loneliness problem is caused by of Required Masculinity, you have to break the grip of its many anti-friendship rules. Okay, you say, I walk away from it, and then what? Good relationships need honest people and emotions. How are you going to find these? You need to start selecting and practicing your own masculinity Tools and Intentions (Challenges #2 to #4). And, you'll need to replace your emotional ignorance with emotional intelligence (Challenge #5).

Common conversation talks often about "finding" a relationship, as if it were an empty soda bottle along the street, a paper napkin tossed from a passing car, a blooming trillium found alongside a woodland path, or a book in the library. Relationships are not found, and they do not descend from a star or sit on the fingertips of an interplanetary being. For all of us, men and women like, each relationship is built bit by bit, consciously, and with careful intention and creative effort. The process is much like a scientist's lab experiment or an artist's piece of creativity. It's try, try, try again, each time changing something or finding something new about your Self or your friend's Self. When you get good feedback and feel solid ground under a relationship, slow down, pay close attention, and practice and practice this good feedback. A relationship is never built once and for all, since you keep changing and so does the person you're building this relationship with and so does the world around the two of you. It needs constant intention and attention, constant tweeks and up-dating.

Can Men Have Deep Male Friendships?

The gay man's experience of being "in the closet" is replicated to an astonishing degree these days by a straight man trying to maintain a deep male friendship. Few people are told of his male friend, and even fewer are introduced to him, any activity with him and word of their friendship is rarely shared, and the male friend is often little more than a mystery person to a man's wife and children, who don't ask about him although his wife might resent the friend. There's not even a word for this man in English. "Boy friend"? All the wrong connotations. "Man friend"? Better, but nasty, homophobic questions dangle from it. "Intimate friend"? This drips sex. Deep and personal conversations, if they are had at all, are wrapped in any feasible excuse, e.g., building something or moving something or watching sports. How different this is from a woman's female friends, whom she talks about openly and regularly.

Regardless of these obstacles, we know that such male friendships are possible. You probably know several strong and deep friendships between men and may even have experienced one. If we could only investigate these friendships, I'm very sure that we would uncover all kinds of Personal Masculinity Tools and Intentions these men used to build and maintain their friendship. Even if we find these Tools and Intentions and put them to use, deep male friendship will still face the homophobic challenges of Required Masculinity and our culture.

Building a deep male friendship won't be easy for us the first few times, since we have limited knowledge, experience, or models to follow. On the other hand, strong motivation, opportunity, and effort are often very good mentors. Patience and quiet insistence also help two men build their friendship deeply. A men's support group or a Men's Weekend can also give you a safe place to begin and may introduce you to good models to follow. Here and there, we're beginning to see more traces of close male friendships. A man's arm slung casually over his male friend's shoulder in quiet, casual moments. Men hugging each other on meeting or separating, instead of the distancing handshake. Whatever your efforts, this friendship will be absolutely worth it.

Can My Father Be My Friend?

Almost every man I have heard talk about his father wished that he and his father were deep friends, even if his father had been abusive or absent in the man's youth. Regardless of this strongly felt wish, very few men apparently find this. So much stands in their way: the friendship barriers in Required Masculinity, work hours, commuting distances, emotional repression, the mother's defense of "her children", the parent-child hierarchy, a father's lack of close experience with children. Without any doubt, there is still a strong bias in our culture against deep, active fathering, although a steady stream of recent research argues strongly for the value of fathering and, sometimes, its necessity. Slowly, for very determined fathers, fully-grown fathering beyond dispensing money and discipline is gaining ground, but our culture still seems only barely tolerant of it. See Challenge #8.

According to the stories shared in my groups, penetrating these obstacles needs a lot of luck and the stars lined up the right way. In many cases I heard about, the son-father friendship began unexpectedly as the result of one of them saying something slightly out of the expected in a quiet moment together or finding themselves caught on the same side in some crisis or family argument. The best advice I can give you for getting a relationship started with your father is to use the knowledge and skills you've acquired over the years to help him in some moment of his need, providing these with as little comment as you would to any fellow worker in need. His realizing that you have skills and wisdom useful to him seems to go a long way to breaking that parent-child hierarchy. Be alert for this opening when it comes, and then be gentle and patient in nurturing this friendship. Some of the best stories I've heard were when a son ignored everything from their past and kept the conversation focused on getting the father's present need met. Keep in mind that you are both trying to climb two hills at the same time: father-son and male friendship. I wish that I could share a first-hand experience in building a deep friendship with my father, but, by the time I was ready and able to try this, my father had been dead for over twenty-five years.

Every man I've heard talk about a strong friendship with his father speaks of it with deep satisfaction and excitement. These feelings seem particularly strong when father and son work out their friendship in spite of past father-son tensions or abuse. I've heard amazing stories in my groups about these friendships overcoming long abuse or abandonment histories and deep philosophical or political differences. Seeing each other as just men struggling to live with the same issues and stresses lets you respect each other and, on occasion, learn from each other and feel less that you each are the only man stupid enough or incompetent enough or unlucky enough to have your struggles. The most moving father-son stories I've heard are when a son experiences his father crying. The emotion behind these tears seems to speak volumes to both father and son, and opens a closeness they both often desperately want.

CHALLENGE # 8:
BEING A FATHER

"Good father" is defined by Paul Raeburn in his *Do Fathers Matter? What Science Is Telling Us About The Parent We've Overlooked* (2014) in a number of ways. The research Raeburn discusses makes it very clear that "good fathering" is about the quantity and quality of time you spend with your child. Another piece of this fathering is that both mother and father are consistent and peaceful in their parenting, This latter requires that the mother and you have a mutually accepted, and mutually built, plan of parenting. Mark O'Connell, in *The Good Father*, proposes a different view of the "good father", one that is broader in scope. The core of this view is that a father should be authoritative but not authoritarian. An authoritative father is one who shows his knowledge, skills, and experience firmly and confidently and uses them for the benefit of the child. An authoritarian father is one who demands obedience to his orders and choices, making him very close to the standard Required Masculinity male. Daily fathering, of course, has to deal with endless and constantly shifting details, so, ultimately, good fathering lies in you being responsive to these details.

Opting out of the elements of Required Masculinity will certainly help you be a good father. If the masculinity Tools and Intentions you choose to express include components related to emotions, cooperation, relationships, creativity, freedom, and respect, your choices will certainly help you be a good father to your daughter or son. As you choose your Personal Masculinity and learn to express it, you also develop confidence in your own choices and the strength to live them honestly. These abilities will also make you a more confident father. This confidence will also help you confront the No Fathers Wanted barriers we discuss next and may well get you over them. Expressing your own Tools and Intentions will give your children, especially your son, a good model to follow in making their choices along the way from baby to adult. Turning the fathering subject around, these same abilities will probably also help you build a better connection with your own father, which we discussed in the last Challenge.

Nobody Wants Me To Father Actively

You're right. You and all men face major opposition to being an active father. Required Masculinity says, "Children is women's work." Social pressure says, "A man's only job is to earn money for his family." The nearly all-powerful media makes fun of the whole idea of a man even attempting to take care of his children. Between sixty and eighty percent of mothers actively oppose men getting involved with "my" children (*Do Fathers Matter*, 218). Most of these same women, however, complain bitterly in the research that they are angry at their husbands for not participating in child care. Hypocrisy? Blindness? You guess. Or, maybe they just want feeding and diaper changing robots and not substantive fathering.

Given the long history of fathering and of men teaching their sons the family trade, all of this current opposition to fathering looks very strange. Without some full-scale research, we're left with just speculation as an answer for this change. Does Required Masculinity make men so dangerous to the welfare of children that mothers push fathers out of the house to protect their children? Were the mothers so jealous of the domestic power the men claimed because they brought home the money, that they made the children "my children" so that they could shut the door on the men in retaliation? Who knows. In any event, the answer would probably not help you climb over this opposition to active fathering.

Another form of this anti-fathering hurdle, however, is employer resistance to giving fathers un-penalized time to be fathers. Even with the slowly rising social acceptance of active fathering, most employers still feel totally within their rights and needs to push work demands into every home and family. This takes many forms: compulsory overtime, often unscheduled; 24/7 phone and computer access; extensive travel; work hours that remove the father from his children's normal schedules. Tamping down these demands to something like a fair balance of work and family is often impossible. I can't provide you, I'm sorry to say, with any effective suggestions to solve this. Some of the research in *Do Fathers Matter* might be persuasive, but corporate policy seems impervious to mere facts. Asking for more fathering time will at least be better than just letting your employer go on its classic anti-fathering way unchallenged. If enough fathers ask directly and publicly for fathering time, change may come, but probably only after your children are grown, unfortunately.

You will face yet another form of this anti-fathering hurdle should you and your wife or partner separate and you want to gain joint custody of your children. This will be the family court and child welfare systems. The courts and child-welfare agencies and organizations are notoriously pro-mother and, if not actively anti-father, then intent on ignoring fathers or twisting the emotions and goals of the multiple players in the separation or divorce against the father. Some people claim that this antagonism towards fathers is waning. The fathers' rights organizations, though, still see more than enough current anti-fathering in these systems to stay active. These forces are exacerbated when you and the mother fight between yourselves or try to use your children as allies or hidden agents. If ever, a parenting plan in a divorce or separation situation MUST put the welfare of the children first. Given the strength of the egos and pressures involved in divorce and custody clashes, finding and following a plan can be very difficult to accomplish and will be one of the heaviest tests of your fathering desires.

Only in the last few decades or so have serious efforts been made to tear down this anti-fathering hurdle, though it doesn't seem to have been lowered by much. So, you'll have to climb over it. Don't treat this as a cultural condition you have to wait for time and a shifting universe to change; treat it as your family's own challenge. Work out with your wife or partner a clear place and time for your fathering, using a written parenting plan if necessary. Before you have this discussion with the mother of your child, it could be useful for you to do some serious study about parenting, child development, and fathering. Try to prepare yourself on two fronts: facts and arguments supporting the importance to your child's development of having an active father, and what specifically you want to do for and with your particular child. Both the Raeburn and O'Connell books will give you a wide variety of evidence and ideas to persuade a skeptical or resistant mother to accept your fathering intentions.

What Is Best For My Children

Do Dominance Competition, power, control, and the rest of the elements of Required Masculinity sound like good Tools to use with your child, that your child will respond to well? If not, then once again you need something other than Required Masculinity.

Raeburn strongly urges "quality time" as a good fathering technique. With a young child, this primarily means play time, the more physical and the more different from the child's daily routine the better. The direction for this is best coming from your child as much as from you. Once your child is in school, good fathering is knowing and talking about what your child is doing and learning, who her friends are, and what intrigues him. Good fathering is also about making sure your child feels, even when you are disciplining him, that you always accept him as he is. If the child feels regularly rejected or negatively judged by one or both of her parents, the results are usually juvenile delinquency, early sexual activity, and the addiction road. Yes, good fathering sometimes does require stiff and inflexible rules and enforcement, but a "good father" keeps these to the rare times when your child is in real danger.

Raeburn also reports research showing that fathers make big contribution to their children by leading them into experiences that give them the skills and confidence to operate successfully in the world outside of home, especially in school. Specifically:

Vocabulary development

Getting along with strangers and making friends

Dealing with unknowns and surprises

Taking risks for new learning experiences

One of the most counter-intuitive conclusions I read in *Do Fathers Matter* is that a man playing physically and imaginatively with his young child gives the child these specific skills. This result, however, is backed by other research as well. This play can include almost anything: reading aloud, especially books that stretch the child's experience; taking them to a new environment or into a totally foreign feeling, e.g., sailboat or horse; asking her to design your joint play time, and then playing it her way; the classic "horsie" games that have been played by fathers and children for eons; trips to the office, the mall, the park, the church. Your options are endless. The research implies that play is not something just for 2-5 year olds; it is valuable for children of all ages. My children, now in their forties, still talk about the big trip each of them had with my mother when they were each around twelve and the impact it had on them. The research says that the best activities are those that create fun shared by both you and your child, give a sense of freedom from the "usual rules", and present challenges to the "usual" in the child's life.

O'Connell does not focus on specific fathering activities, but on broad psychological needs for both child and father. This information offers you a variety of Tools to apply and the endless variety of situations you will move through as you raise your daughter or son.

Paul Raeburn, *Do Fathers Matter? What Science Is Telling Us About The Parent We've Overlooked,* 2014.

Mark O'Connell, *The Good Father: On Men, Masculinity, and Life in the Family,* 2005, Scribner.

PART 3

BEING THE MAN I WANT TO BE

It's time to stop reading. It's time to start making your decisions about your masculinity Tools and Intentions. My job is done. It's up to you now.

"But, but, but," I hear you sputtering, "my life doesn't look like any of this stuff." Oh, really? Have I, then, pulled all this information out of thin air? How much of what I have described to you on these pages can you honestly say that you have never seen, or heard, or felt in your bones? Have you never heard yourself asking, "How much power, control, money, and sex do I actually want?" "Why can't I be what I want to be?" Have you never watched, enviously, as a friend or work mate jumps in a sailboat and heads for the horizon? Or, becomes a horse rancher just because he loves horses and the outdoors?

It's time to take off the Required Masculinity glasses that show you only one way to be masculine and look at all of the other masculinities available to you. It's time to take your life away from the tyrant and live it the way that's your way. Walking out of this box voluntarily gives you the confidence and time to find your Self and build your Personal Masculinity at your own pace. Certainly, you can wait. At some point, though, job loss, divorce, major illness, accident, fire, financial collapse, or a significant loss of any kind will rip these old glasses off you. Then, you'll have to do your finding and building in the midst of chaos and fear with time at a minimum. The sooner you start the walk from Required Masculinity to your Personal Masculinity, the sooner you'll get to the life that feels like really living.

We all know that breaking habits and finding new ways isn't easy. *You* have to start, and *you* have to keep at it. Don't beat yourself up for occasional failures, delays, or oversights on your part; these are totally normal and, with continued practice and attention, they will disappear. Everything in this book, your various scribbles on its pages, and your answers to the questions in Appendix 1 give you many roads to follow to finding and expressing your Self, your Tools and Intentions, and your Personal Masculinity.

Get started. Now.

EXPLORATION QUESTIONS

What does "masculinity" mean to you?

What questions do you want to ask of masculinity?

What would you like to understand more clearly about *your* masculinity by the time you close this book?

Name five situations in the last week in which you expressed the tools and intentions of Required Masculinity.

1.

2.

3.

4.

5.

Identify the lesson about Required Masculinity you learned from each of these experiences.

1.

2.

3.

4.

5.

What costs did you pay by making each of these Required Masculinity choices?

1.

2.

3.

4.

5.

Think about three conflicts that you have recently faced. How did Required Masculinity help or hinder the resolution of these conflicts?

1.

2.

3.

What methods would you have preferred to use to process the conflicts you just listed?

1.

2.

3.

How could you have successfully introduced your preferred conflict response methods into one of these conflicts?

List four events which have enforced Required Masculinity on you.

1.

2.

3.

4.

List three people who were or are the most insistent that you be a Required Masculinity Male.

1.

2.

3.

Why *can't* you leave Required Masculinity? Write down the three strongest reasons:

1.

2.

3.

Which three masculinities models discussed in pages 104-119 are most attractive to you?

1.

2.

3.

Put a big check mark in front of the one you rate the most attractive for you right now.

What Tools and Intentions of Required Masculinity do you want in your own masculinity?

What will these Tools and Intentions gain you?

What will these Tools and Intentions cost you?

What elements in your Self Profile do you most want to express regularly?

What in your work encourages your Personal Masculinity choices?

Can you think of ways to expand this encouragement or, if nothing encourages it, ways for you to express your Personal Masculinity anyway?

What are your three biggest fears about your own emotions?

1.

2.

3.

Which emotion that you've ever experienced do you understand least? What would you like to know about this emotion?

Name three emotions in other people that you felt in the last three days that you didn't feel comfortable responding to.

1.

2.

3.

Carl Erikson

Name three things you want from a close friendship.

1.

2.

3.

Name three men and women from any time in your life that you would like to have had a deep friendship with?

What would have been the most important elements of each of these friendships for you?

What would you like a close friendship with your father to be like?

Think of two ways for you to help your son expand his vocabulary and its use that will interest him.

1.

2.

Think of two unusual ways for you to help your daughter learn to interact usefully with the world that will interest her.

1.

2.

Think of two experiences to lead your child into that will be totally new to him or her.

1.

2.

APPENDIX 2

TOPICS

APPENDIX 3

SUGGESTED READING

REQUIRED MASCULINITY

Brain Sex, Ann Moir and David Jessel, Dell Publishing, 1991.

From Chivalry to Terrorism: War and the Changing Nature of Masculinity, Leo Braudy, Alfred A. Knopf, 2003.

The End of Man and The Rise of Women, Hanna Rosin, Penguin Group, 2012.

The Good Son, Michael Gurian, Penguin Putnam Inc, 1999.

Guyland, Michael Kimmel, Harper Collins, 2008

History of Masculinity, R.W. Connell, University of California Press, 1995.

The Irritable Male Syndrome, Jed Diamond, Rodale Press, 2004.

Man Enough: Fathers, Sons, and the Search for Masculinity, Frank Pittman, G.P. Putnam, 1993.

Manhood in America – A Cultural History, Michael Kimmel, The Free Press, 1996.

The Masculine Self, Third Edition, Christopher T. Kilmartin, Sloan Publishing, 2007.

The Myth of Male Power, Warren Farrell, Simon and Schuster, 1993.

The Professor in the Cage: Why Men Fight and Why We Like to Watch, Jonathan Gottschall,
Penguin Press, 2015.

Real Boys, William Pollack, Henry Holt & Company, 1998.

Real Boys' Voices, William Pollack with Todd Shuster, Random House, 2000.

Voice Male, a quarterly magazine touching on many issues of boys and men. Voicemalemagazine.org

Voice Male: The Untold Story of the Profeminist Men's Movement, ed. Rob Okun. Interlink Publishing Group, 2014. This contains many articles from the magazine.

Why Men Are the Way They Are, Warren Farrell, McGraw Hlll, 1986.

CRITICISM OF REQUIRED MASCULINITY

The Bully Society: School Shootings and the Crisis of Bullying in America's Schools, Jesse Klein, New York University Press, 2012. This also discusses bullying at work.

The Decline of Men: How the American Male is Tuning out, Giving Up, and Flipping Off His Future, Guy Garcia, Harper Collins Publishers, 2008.

Delusions of Gender: How our minds, society and neuro-sexism create difference, Cordelia Fine, W.W. Norton & Company, 2010.

Stiffed – The Betrayal of the American Man, Susan Faludi, William Morrow, 1999.

OTHER MASCULINITIES

Breaking Out, The 48 Laws of Power, Robert Greene, Penguin Books, 1998.

The Craftsman, Richard Sennet, Yale University Press, 2008.

The Masculine Self, Christopher Kilmartin, Sloan Publishing, 2007.

The Path of the Green Man, Gay men, Wicca and Living a Magical Life, Michael Thomas Ford, Citadel Press, 2005.

The Promise of a Pencil: How an Ordinary Person can Create Extraordinary Change, Adam Brown, Scribners, 2014

The Renaissance Soul, Margaret Lobenstine, Broadway Books, 2006.

Self-Made Man, Norah Vincent, Penguin Books, 2006.

Shop Class As Soulcraft: An Inquiry Into the Value of Work, Matthew Crawford, The Penguin Press, 2009.

Unlocking The Iron Cage: The Men's Movement, Gender Politics, and American Culture, Michael Schwalter, Oxford University Press. 1996.

You'll See It When You Believe It, Wayne Dyer, William Morrow and Company, 1989.

What is a Man? – 3000 years of wisdom on the art of manly virtue, ed. Waller Newell, Regan Books, 2001.

The Will to Change, bell hooks, Atria Books, 2004.

Why We Make Things and Why It Matters: The Education of a Craftsman, Peter Korn, David Godine Publisher, 2013.

EMOTIONS

Emotional Intelligence: Why it can matter more than I, Daniel Goleman, Bantam Books, 1995.

LONELINESS

Loneliness: Human Nature and the Need for Social Connection, John Cacioppo and William Patrick, W.W. Norton & Company, 2008

FATHERING

Do Fathers Matter? What Science Is Telling Us about The Parent we've Overlooked, Paul Raeburn, Farrar Straus & Giroux, 2014

Father Courage: What happens when men put family first, Suzanne Brown Levine, Harcourt Inc, 2000.

The Good Father: On Men, Masculinity, and Life in the Family, Mark O'Connell, 2005, Scribner.

Printed in the United States
By Bookmasters